Helping Hands

A Support Group Manual for the Divorced, Widowed or Separated

JAMES L. HORSTMAN AND VAN T. MOON

PAULIST PRESS

New York/Mahwah

Book design by Nighthawk Design.

ISBN: 0-8091-3399-7

Published by Paulist Press
997 Macarthur Boulevard
Mahwah, New Jersey 07430

Printed and bound in the United States of America

Contents

PROGRAMS

Icebreakers

Grief

Self-Esteem

Spiritual Growth

Forgiveness

Sexuality

Trust

Parenting

Special Problems

Values

Fun in General

Acknowledgments

There were many people who contributed their support and encouragement to the writing of this manual—so many that it is impossible to list all of them. But our thanks goes out to all of them for their efforts, knowledge, and resources.

There are some, however, without whom this manual could not have been completed. First is Father Joel Gromowski, C.P. (deceased). A Passionist priest (he sure was), and it was out of his compassion that an idea gained form and began to function. It was his support and encouragement that enabled all others to keep on going.

Our thanks also goes out to Tommy Tidemann for the special effort she added. Her total personality kept the effort from becoming a drudgery. Her humor, her love for others, and her deep-seated concern for those hurting left its mark on this project.

Thanks also to Sandy Baumer for her many talents and abilities: deep feelings, honest approach, spiritual depth and a vast amount of knowledge about almost everything. Sandy's ideas kept overcoming defeat and boredom. She could sense problems before anyone else, move to overcome them, and not let them take hold and become overwhelming. She personified the totality of the idea: to create, serve and solve.

Thanks also to Marcie Oberhoff who assisted in the editing of this manual. Her experience filled an important void.

Foreword

It is with great joy and thankfulness that I welcome this book into the field of resources and helps for those ministering to the separated, divorced, and widowed. I applaud the authors for their empowering collection of themes and questions, prayer and scriptural texts. They understand the starting point of support group ministry and gift us with their experience and research, learning and spirituality.

What is particularly attractive about this book is its versatility—its capacity to work within the wide range of group models available today. It does not impose restrictions; it can be effective within each group's style. The book provides variety and direction for beginning and sustaining support groups, offers concise advice about how to proceed, and opens new areas and discussion styles.

From the correspondence I receive, it is obvious that the primary need of support group leaders is information on group planning and leadership style. The "What should we do?" and "How should we do it?" questions concern new leaders and veterans. I view this book as an effective answer to those questions.

Kathy Kircher
Former Executive Director
North American Conference for
Separated and Divorced Catholics

Introduction

ABOUT THE AUTHORS

Jim Horstman

As a divorced father of three, Jim brings first-hand knowledge to his ministerial programs. Jim currently works for the Galveston-Houston Diocese as Director of Ministry to the Divorced, Widowed, and Separated. He serves as a board member on The Diocesan Board of Pastoral Care, The North American Conference of Separated and Divorced Catholics, Community of Daybreak, and the San Jose Clinic. He also served on the Professional Advisory Board for the North American Conference of Separated and Divorced Catholics, and on the Board of the Community of Daybreak. Jim writes articles, presents a self-help program "WINNING," gives lectures, assists the local support groups, leads a workshop for training ministry leadership, serves as an advocate for the Diocesan Tribunal, and, in his spare time, works with abused and neglected children.

Jim is a member of the NACSDC, a member and former chancellor of the Knight of Columbus, a member and president of his parish men's organization, and a eucharistic minister. He is a graduate of Eastern Illinois University, a speaker, lecturer, and writer.

Van T. Moon

Van is a divorced father of five sons. He first attended a Beginning Experience weekend in 1981. Two weeks later he volunteered to serve in the divorced ministry. He became active on three different support groups and began taking Bible study courses. In 1982 Van participated, as the Catholic representative, in the Episcopal Church training for the divorced. That same year he served on the core team of his parish support group and on the Advisory Board for the divorced and widowed for the diocese. In 1983 he organized and wrote the constitution for the newly formed Diocesan Board of Pastoral Care for the Divorced, Separated, and Widowed (The Compassion Ministry). He then served as the board's first chairman in 1983 and 1984. Also in 1983 and 1984 he was treasurer for Arise and Walk Conference and has given workshops for them and for NACSDC Region 10.

Van said that after he received his annulment, he thought that the process was as rough as the divorce. So he submitted a proposal to the Tribunal office to form an Advocate Program to train lay people to help the divorced prepare papers and forms for the annulment process. The program proved very successful and is now a model for other dioceses.

Van has attended the Effective Living Seminar, he teaches "Listening Skills" to new facilitators, and he gives talks and workshops to groups on various topics. Van has taught Bible study courses and is presently a lector in his parish, serves on the R.C.I.A. team and is a member of the liturgy committee. Van is a graduate of the University of Oklahoma. In addition to all his many activities, Van finds time to practice "Hug Therapy." He gives great hugs.

WHY THIS BOOK WAS WRITTEN

This program guide started out to be just a few programs that could fill in some voids for existing support groups. However, high turnover, change of leadership, and the question "How can we start and maintain a support group?" provided a challenge and a new direction for the guide. We heard from existing groups that were having trouble retaining old members and losing new members who didn't come back. We heard from churches that wanted to form a support group but had little or no idea of how to get started. The little literature that existed on the subject was scattered piecemeal through hundreds of volumes. The Galveston-Houston Diocese was deluged with questions about the successful groups here. Each question seemed to point to a new area that needed to be covered.

Obviously someone needed to combine enough information into one volume to answer some of these questions. Therefore this book was born. Although one book cannot be the answer to all the problems, we hope this book will help.

WHAT IS A SUPPORT GROUP?

According to Webster, to support is "to hold up or serve as a foundation or prop; to keep from fainting, yielding, or losing courage; to comfort." A group is "two or more units forming a complete entity, a number of individuals assembled together or having some unifying relationship."

A support group is nothing more than several people who meet to help each other and, in so doing, help themselves as well. Members can talk and share feelings with those who are suffering and struggling through the pains of death or a broken marriage. They find out that they are not alone, that others have experienced those same problems and survived, and even have grown mentally and spiritually in the process. Support group members help each other to find answers within themselves and with God. They help each other to find God's healing touch. With compassion, love, and true concern for one another, they share the good times and the bad, the smiles and the tears.

WHEN DO WE NEED SUPPORT GROUPS?

When relationships end, we feel separated from others. Isolated within ourselves, we feel unloved and desolate. We get angry with God; we feel saddened and experience a sense of loss. We long for companionship and support.

God did not intend us to feel alone, and he does not want us to continue to suffer. Through his unconditional love and the Holy Spirit he uses us to create support groups. Through his love and compassion he has given us a place to gather and to begin a new life, surrounded by the gift of others.

HOW DO WE START A SUPPORT GROUP?

The ways of starting a support group are as many and as different as the number of existing groups. We hope that these guidelines will help.

I. Tell your pastor of your desire to start a support group and enlist his help.

II. Set a place, day, and time for a first meeting (allow three weeks to prepare).

III. Advertise your intentions.

A. Write an announcement that the pastor can deliver at church.

B. Advertise in a local or area newsletter or newspaper.

C. Use free radio or TV announcements (talk shows, etc.).

D. Publicize your desire through the church council and staff.

E. Look for help through your church structure and other religious institutions.

F. Tell everyone about your intentions—at the office, at the supermarket, in the neighborhood, anywhere.

IV. Prepare a sign-in sheet to use at the first meeting. Ask for the following information:

A. name, address, and telephone number

B. marital status

C. how long

D. number of children

E. whether children are with you or with ex-spouse

F. work

G. hobbies

When you hold the first meeting, let all those attending introduce themselves, briefly including some of the above information. Use the program named Icebreaker #1. After completing it, announce the place, day, and time of the next two meetings and the programs you'll have.

Repeat the same steps for the second meeting, this time using the program named Icebreaker #2.

The third meeting will be your organization and business meeting. Follow all the above steps. Have an opening prayer and a scripture reading. However, for the program, present the following list of necessary jobs:

1. Coordinator (chair and vice-chair)
The coordinator conducts meetings of members and the core team or executive committee, arranges for facilities for meetings, provides a business agenda, and communicates with other support groups.

2. Secretary and historian-librarian
The secretary builds and maintains a library of books, tapes, and periodicals, takes minutes and keeps records, keeps a scrapbook of photos or events, writes confirmations and thank-you notes to speakers, sends get-well cards and birthday cards to members, and performs other writing chores as needed.

3. Treasurer and program chairperson
The treasurer arranges for a program or a speaker, arranges for any materials or equipment needed, introduces the program or the speaker, conducts the group program, assesses the needs of the group to select programs, keeps money and accounting, pays bills for supplies or speakers, collects and reports status of funds, and arranges for an assessment or a pass-the-hat for group financial needs.

4. Membership and telephone
The membership person keeps an up-to-date membership list at all times, oversees a telephone committee that calls all new members for at least two meetings, calls absent members after two meetings, calls the core team or executive committee for meetings, calls members for emergency meetings, and supervises a table that contains a sign-in sheet, name tags, and handout materials.

5. Newsletter and publicity
The newsletter person researches and writes interesting articles, prepares a monthly or bimonthly newsletter that includes meeting information, speakers, social events, articles, etc., prints and distributes the newsletter, and communicates with other groups and media.

6. Hospitality and refreshments
The hospitality person provides refreshments, welcomes people, paying special attention to new members, visits sick members, and encourages attendance for all functions.

7. Social and baby sitting
The social person arranges for baby-sitting as needed, and plans and organizes all social functions, such as dances, theatre trips, etc.

Depending on the size and number of members, the jobs can be separated or further combined as needed.

After you explain the jobs and descriptions, ask for volunteers to fill these positions for at least six months. Explain that the core team or executive committee will decide, sometime in the next six months, how the positions are to be filled in the future. (Some choices are: election, volunteers, drafting, or assigning.) Have a closing prayer at the end of the meeting.

Cautions:

A. Do not let the leaders be chosen strictly by a popularity contest. Fit the person who has the talents and abilities to the job. It takes all kinds of people and special talents to successfully run a support group. Each job is an honor, and it is the total efforts of all the leadership that will result in a good functioning support group.

B. Do not let the leaders become entrenched in a particular job, or view the job as a ladder to the "top position." Each job is a top position and deserves the best results. Always be on the lookout for new people who have those special talents. This helps to prevent stagnation and suffocation within the support group.

V. Now you are off and running. You have had two Icebreaker meetings to get acquainted, so some people with organizational and leadership skills should have emerged. Recruit them for the first term officers (core team). The core team should meet before the next general meeting to arrange agenda, program needs, financial reports, etc., so that the meeting can run more efficiently.

How To Use This Manual

THE STRUCTURE OF THE MANUAL

This book was written to offer guidance on some of the problems experienced by the divorced, widowed, and separated. These programs are not intended to be final answers. Rather, they are meant as a starting point, a place that people can begin to find their own solutions.

In this book you'll find a definition of support group, advice on starting a group, and a list of reading materials. The list, arranged alphabetically by title, includes books on self-help topics, books that promote spiritual growth, books specifically for the divorced or widowed, and books that foster leadership.

If you do not have access to a support group and want to start one, use the information in the section entitled "How To Start a Support Group." If, however, you already have an active group, you can turn immediately to the section entitled "Programs." You can use this reservoir of programs when you have limited time, limited facilities, or limited personnel. The program section starts with two icebreakers. The other programs are divided into ten topics:

Grief	Trust
Self-Esteem	Parenting
Spiritual Growth	Fun in General
Forgiveness	Special Problems
Sexuality	Values

These programs are not presented in a particular order; use them in the order that best suits the needs of your group. Each program begins with a five part format. The program notes which follow the five-part format may be xeroxed. (Be sure to make a few extras for new people who might appear.)

The programs in this book all follow the same five-part format. Each begins with an opening prayer. You can use the one provided, or use another if you desire. Next comes the business meeting. This portion includes announcements of group activities, the treasurer's report, and other items of group interest. Keep the business meeting as short as possible.

A scripture reading is the third part of the outline. The Bible reading given with each program was chosen especially to fit the theme of that program. However you can substitute other verses if you feel that they are more appropriate. Next comes the actual program. Before passing out copies of the program sheet, tell everyone to wait until each member has received a copy before starting to read. When you've handed everyone a copy, read through the program with the group and then tell them to answer the questions. (The leader should always participate in the program.) Tell them to write exactly what they feel. No one will see what they write. Explain that they can use the back of the page if they need additional space.

Allow an adequate amount of time to complete the questionnaire. When everyone finishes, tell the group to separate into groups of three to four people each to discuss the questions and answers.

After a reasonable amount of time for discussion in the groups, call the large group together again. Encourage group discussion of the questions and answers. Ask a spokesman from each group to give a summation of what that group discussed and their conclusions.

The last item on the agenda is the closing prayer. Again, one is provided with each program, but you or one of the members can offer another.

GUIDELINES FOR PROGRAM LEADERS

These programs can supplement other programs of your own devising. You do not have to use every program in the book; you can reuse each one as many times as you feel is necessary for your group. However, continued use of the programs in this book can eventually become boring, causing your members to lose interest in the group. A balance of topics is essential to keep continued interest. You must know your people and where they are. You can choose a topic by evaluation of your group's needs or through voting by the group. Select topics that fit the majority of your members, keeping in mind that the personality of any group changes each time a new member is added.

Keep your programs as varied as possible. Use topics from many resources to add spice to your meetings; you can use speakers, social events, self-help, special interests (for instance, "How To Change the Oil in Your Car" or "How To Sew on a Button"). As a group leader you should keep in mind that the needs of those in trauma are greater than the needs of those who have begun the healing process. Their topics should be given greater priority because of their greater needs. It is important to minister to those who need it most, those who are hurting the most, whether they be new or old members. Your group should recognize that all people have a right to be received with their experiences and feelings.

If you are using programs from this book, be sure to prepare enough copies of each of the handouts before each meeting. Make a few extra for any visitors that may attend. It is important that you, as program leader, be familiar with all the program topics and the programs covered in each section of this book. You should also make use of the other resources listed at the end of this book.

It is important that your meetings achieve a balance between structure and process so that each group member can move forward with the task of healing, good-byes and new beginnings. Do all that you can to promote active listening by all your members. Remind them that validating each experience is basic to growth.

SUGGESTIONS FOR PROGRAM LEADERS

1. Limit each small group to four to six people. This will give each person time to talk and keep your meeting within its time limits.

2. The leader should manage the time for the groups. Some will use two or three minutes per person and some will need more time. Do not let one person dominate or monopolize the time.

3. Do not let anyone pass moral or intellectual judgments on the group or other participants in the group. Sharing should be absolutely confidential within the group or the depth of sharing will be sacrificed. Inspire acceptance to love and compassion; be empathetic; encourage people to put themselves in the other person's place.

4. Listen to the other person's story and feelings objectively. Everyone has to be able to tell his or her story; this is where the healing nature of sharing will take place. Do not allow yourself or others to analyze or diagnose what others have said.

5. Recognize that all those in the group are in a different place from one another. Do not press for more details. Ask what they are feeling. Do not put them down for what they say. Build them up; accept rather than reject. There is nothing that God cannot forgive, and if he can forgive so should you.

6. Be especially sensitive to newcomers. Recognize that most of them will feel estranged, not yet accepted, and reluctant to share. Be patient, understanding, encouraging and compassionate. Newcomers usually will have a hard time joining in the sharing (remember, it was a major step for them just to come). Wait for them to feel ready.

Always be aware that God sustains us in our efforts to resolve painful conflicts and helps to heal the heartbreak that usually accompanies the end of marriage.

Icebreakers

Getting To Know Myself

I. Opening Prayer

Lord, thank you for walking with me through life, not only up the hills, but through the valleys. You were there when I went through the desert; you were there when I walked over green fields. You were there when I loved others; you were there when I didn't. You were there when I was happy and smiling, and you sat beside me when I wept. Thank you, Lord; you have been beside me all along. Amen.

II. Business Report

III. Scripture Reading: Psalm 122:6–9

Pray for the peace of Jerusalem! May those who love you prosper! May peace be within your buildings. Because of my relatives and friends I will say, "Peace be within you!" Because of the house of the Lord, our God, I will pray for your good.

IV. Program

The program notes begin on the next page. You are encouraged to build on these ideas. However, each program is self-contained and can be used exactly as is if you desire. Refer to the section entitled "How To Use This Manual" for guidelines on conducting the program.

V. Closing Prayer

Dear Father, we give eternal thanks to you for all the blessings you have given us, for the health we enjoy, for our homes, for our jobs. We give thanks for the Holy Spirit whom you gave to us to guide us, lead us, and pick us up when we stumble or fall. We know that you, in your mercy and love, will bring good out of our trials and tribulations. Let these experiences cause us to grow in our trust and love of you. Help us to accept your will in our lives and to submit our will to you. Amen.

A. Answer the following questions.

1. Around people I don't know, I am usually (circle two):

a. Mr. (Ms.) Super Cool   g. clumsy

b. nervous   h. a little uptight

c. quiet   i. the liberated woman (man)

d. outgoing   j. the life of the party

e. goosey   k. all thumbs

f. confident   l. other _____

2. Three qualities I look for in a friend are (rank 1, 2, 3, etc.):

_____ honesty	_____ placidity	
_____ openness	_____ brown eyes	
_____ understanding	_____ spiritual depth	
_____ loyalty	_____ good looks	
_____ warmth	_____ compatibility	
_____ compassion	_____ sharp dresser	
_____ fun	_____ moral guts	
_____ muscles	_____ social prestige	
_____ personality	_____ popularity	
_____ sense of humor	_____ money	

B. Break into small groups to discuss the preceding exercise.

Looking at Myself

I. Opening Prayer

Father, because your spirit is active in my life as it was in Christ's resurrection, my heart is filled with happiness and praise for you. With strength received from your eternal love and grace, I will conquer the troubles and challenges that stand in my way. Amen.

II. Business Report

III. Scripture Reading: 1 John 1:3–6

What we have seen and heard we proclaim in turn to you so that you may share life with us. This fellowship of ours is with the Father and with his Son, Jesus Christ. Indeed, our purpose in writing you this is that our joy may be complete. Here, then, is the message we have heard from him and announce to you: that God is light; in him there is no darkness. If we say, "We have fellowship with him," while continuing to walk in darkness, we are liars and do not act in truth.

IV. Program

The program notes begin on the next page. You are encouraged to build on these ideas. However, each program is self-contained and can be used exactly as is if you desire. Refer to the section entitled "How To Use This Manual" for guidelines on conducting the program.

V. Closing Prayer

Heavenly Father, thank you for the gift of new friends, because friends are terribly important to us now. We look to them for loyalty and love, for understanding and acceptance. May we accept our new friends and give of ourselves to them when they are in need. Your gift of friendship is always a help to heal our troubled hearts. May we receive this gift from you and may we grow in it, trust in it, and nurture it in the spirit of new love and new life. Amen.

A. Complete the following sentence by circling one choice from each of the twenty-one categories.

I am more like a ———— than a ————.

1. trapeze artist . . . . circus clown

2. sprinter . . . . distance runner

3. television . . . . CB radio

4. magnifying glass . . . . telescope

5. first and ten . . . . goal to goal

6. Johnny Cash . . . . Johnny Carson

7. picture . . . . puzzle

8. candle . . . . light bulb

9. amusement park . . . . library

10. quarterback . . . . blocking back

11. dill pickle . . . . sugar plum

12. dictionary . . . . encyclopedia

13. in the game . . . . on the side

14. golf ball . . . . mush ball

15. hotel . . . . hospital

16. bear . . . . tiger

17. spark plug . . . . battery

18. New York City . . . . Arkansas

19. bridge . . . . tower

20. oak tree. . . . . .evergreen

21. ballet dancer. . . . . .two left feet

B. Break into small groups to discuss the preceding exercise.

Grief

Hurt

I. Opening Prayer

Lord, you know how difficult it is for us to endure suffering and pain, for you know what suffering is like. You, too, suffered much. We pray that you look upon our pain and suffering and we ask that you heal us and ease what we are going through. Help and strengthen us and renew our health and spirit. We ask this through Christ our Lord. Amen.

II. Business Report

III. Scripture Reading: Matthew 27:35–44

When they had crucified him, they divided his clothes among them by casting lots. Then they sat down there and kept watch over him. Above his head they had put the charge against him in writing: "This is Jesus, King of the Jews." Two insurgents were crucified along with him, one at his right and one at his left. People going by kept insulting him, tossing their heads and saying: "So you are the one who was going to destroy the temple and rebuild it in three days! Save yourself, why don't you? Come down off that cross if you are God's Son!" The chief priest, the scribes, and the elders also joined in the jeering: "He saved others but He cannot save himself! So he is the King of Israel! Let's see him come down from that cross and then we will believe in him. He relied on God; let God rescue him now if he wants to. After all, he claimed, 'I am God's Son.'" The insurgents who had been crucified with him kept taunting him in the same way.

IV. Program

The program notes begin on p. 24. You are encouraged to build on these ideas. However, each program is self-contained and can be used exactly as is if you desire. Refer to the section entitled "How To Use This Manual" for guidelines on conducting the program.

V. Closing Prayer

Lord, help me to overcome my feelings of loss and grief. Take the circumstances of my life and use them in a constructive way to do your will. Continue to work patiently with me when I feel there is no hope and I have given up. Stand with me when I am feeling abandoned and alone. Clear my eyes and open my heart; help me live again and let me accept myself and others as you have accepted me with your love. This we ask through Christ our Lord. Amen.

A. Complete the following exercises.

1. Under "HURT," list ten times that you have been hurt (times in your life that you wish were different).

HURT   GROWTH

_____   _____

_____   _____

_____   _____

_____   _____

_____   _____

_____   _____

_____   _____

_____   _____

_____   _____

_____   _____

2. Under "GROWTH," list ten ways that God uses you (things you enjoy doing, your skills, your good times, the person whom you best understand, etc.).

3. Times of hurt often initiate a period of intense growth. Draw a line between the times of hurt and a related area of growth.

4. What growth came the time you were hurt the most?

5. Do you think that this growth made you a better person?

B. Break into small groups to discuss the preceding exercise.

Five Stages of Grief

I. Opening Prayer

Lord, help me to let go of the past and stop clinging to old memories. Take away the regrets and failures that have kept me from seeing the wonder and beauty in my life. The hurts of the past are in the past. Help me to leave them there. Through you I can become a new person, meeting life in a new way. Help me to see the peace and joy that you have sent to fill my life. Through Christ our Lord. Amen.

II. Business Report

III. Scripture Reading: Psalm 126:4–6

Restore our fortunes, O Lord, like the torrents in the southern desert. Those that sow in tears shall reap rejoicing. Although they go forth weeping, carrying the seed to be sown, they shall come back rejoicing, carrying their sheaves.

IV. Program

The program notes begin on the next page. You are encouraged to build on these ideas. However, each program is self-contained and can be used exactly as is if you desire. Refer to the section entitled "How To Use This Manual" for guidelines on conducting the program.

V. Closing Prayer

God, teach me how to walk alone and strong. Heal my wounds and cover my bruises and hurts. Help me to become a single person again, one who is adjusted to new days. Grant me a heart of wisdom. Cleanse me of hostility so that I may know laughter and affection. Keep me from thoughts of despair. Help me to realize that I have closed one section of my life and that I cannot open it again. Help me to move forward in your love and kindness. Amen.

A. Read the following statement.

The five steps of grief are: denial, bargaining, anger, depression, and acceptance.

B. Complete the exercises.

1. What stage was the most difficult for you to resolve?

2. Briefly describe your life situation at the time you felt this stage of grief.

3. How did you feel about the situation?

4. What did you want for yourself? For others?

5. Did you take any action to move yourself from this stage?

6. What action did you take?

7. Looking back at this situation, does it still affect the way you feel about yourself or others?

C. Break into small groups to discuss the above questions and your replies.

Dealing with Grief

I. Opening Prayer

Dear heavenly Father, help us to overcome our destructive feelings. You know that we often carry our hurts and mistakes into bitterness and other feelings that cause us undue grief. We need your help to release these feelings, to learn to call on your forgiveness and let the power of your love take control of our lives. We pray that we will learn to accept what the world has given us, for we know that you do change bad into good. Teach us to have faith in your will and your power. Through Christ our Lord. Amen.

II. Business Report

III. Scripture Reading: John 11:17–33, 38–44

When Jesus arrived at Bethany, he found that Lazarus had already been in the tomb four days. The village was not far from Jerusalem—just under two miles—and many Jewish people had come out to console Martha and Mary over their brother. When Martha heard that Jesus was coming, she went to meet him, while Mary sat at home. Martha said to Jesus, "Lord, if you had been here, my brother would never have died. Even now, I am sure that God will give you whatever you ask of him." "Your brother will rise again," Jesus assured her. "I know he will rise again," Martha replied, "in the resurrection on the last day." Jesus told her: "I am the resurrection and the life: whoever believes in me, though he should die, will come to life; and whoever is alive and believes in me will never die. Do you believe this?" "Yes, Lord," she replied. "I have come to believe that you are the Messiah, the Son of God: he who is to come into the world." When she had said this she went back and called her sister Mary. "The Teacher is here, asking for you," she whispered. As soon as Mary heard this, she got up and started out in his direction. (Actually Jesus had not yet come into the village but was still at the spot where Martha had met him.) The Jews who were in the house with Mary consoling her saw her get up quickly and go out, so they followed her, thinking she was going to the tomb to weep there. When Mary came to the place where Jesus was, seeing him, she fell at his feet and said to him, "Lord, if you had been here my brother would never have died." When Jesus saw her weeping, and the Jews who had accompanied her also weeping, he was troubled in spirit, moved by the deepest emotions. Once again troubled in spirit, Jesus approached the tomb. It was a cave with a stone laid across it. "Take away the stone," Jesus directed. Martha, the dead man's sister, said to him, "Lord it has been four days now; surely there will be a stench!" Jesus replied, "Did I not assure you that if you believed you would see the glory of God displayed?" They then took away the stone and Jesus looked upward and said: "Father, I thank you for having heard me. I know that you always hear me, but I have said this for the sake of the crowd, that they may believe that you sent me." Having said this he called loudly, "Lazarus, come out!" The dead man came out, bound hand and foot with linen strips, his face wrapped in cloth. "Untie him," Jesus told them, "and let him go free."

IV. Program

The program notes begin on the next page. You are encouraged to build on these ideas. However, each program is self-contained and can be used exactly as is if you desire. Refer to the section entitled "How To Use This Manual" for guidelines on conducting the program.

V. Closing Prayer

Dear Lord of all, we thank you for all the blessings you have freely given us—those we too often take for granted, and even those we do not yet accept as blessings. We need your patience and understanding in dealing with life's hurts. Teach us, Father, not to be disturbed by people or situations that we cannot control. Show us how to tune into the law of divine order and divine timing, and how to accept life as you have planned it for us. Amen.

A. Answer the following questions.

1. What are four things in your life that caused you grief?

2. How have these things affected your life-style?

3. How are you presently dealing with the above situations?

B. Break into small groups to discuss the previous exercise.

Alone or Lonely?

I. Opening Prayer

Lord, now that I am a single person, give me the strength to realize that I am alone but need not be lonely. Give me the strength to take risks so that I can find out who I am as an individual, rather than as one-half of a couple. Let me realize that I can grow through my mistakes and weaknesses into a stronger and more loving person. Amen.

II. Business Report

III. Scripture Reading: Hebrews 13:5–6

Do not love money but be content with what you have, for God has said, "I will never desert you, nor will I forsake you." Thus we may say with confidence: "The Lord is my helper, I will not be afraid. What can man do to me?"

IV. Program

The program notes begin on the next page. You are encouraged to build on these ideas. However, each program is self-contained and can be used exactly as is if you desire. Refer to the section entitled "How To Use This Manual" for guidelines on conducting the program.

V. Closing Prayer

Dear Father, help me to learn that I am never really alone because you are always with me. Teach me that I am my own best friend. Give me the ability to use time alone for refreshing my spirit and my love for you. Let me accept that this time is precious and should be wisely used. Amen.

A. Answer the following questions.

1. Do you feel that you have to be part of "a couple" to be happy? Explain your answer briefly.

2. Does your marital status determine your self-worth? How much and why?

3. How does the statement "I feel that I am only half a person" make you feel?

4. Do you feel that you are a failure because your marriage didn't work?

5. What do you think is the difference between being alone and being lonely?

B. Break into small groups to discuss the previous questions.

Reconciliation

I. Opening Prayer

Lord, it hurts so much to see other people going through life so happy when my life seems so shattered. Sometimes I have to fight feelings of anger and jealousy. I react to people in a negative way because of my own pain. Fill me with your peace, Lord. Help me to accept your love and forgiveness and to learn how to love and forgive myself. Amen.

II. Business Report

III. Scripture Reading: Colossians 3:12–16

Because you are God's chosen ones, holy and beloved, clothe yourselves with heartfelt mercy, with kindness, humility, meekness, and patience. Bear with one another; forgive whatever grievances you have against one another. Forgive as the Lord has forgiven you. Over all these virtues put on love, which binds the rest together and makes them perfect. Christ's peace must reign in your hearts, since as members of the one body you have been called to that peace. Dedicate yourselves to thankfulness. Let the word of Christ, rich as it is, dwell in you. In wisdom made perfect, instruct and admonish one another. Sing gratefully to God from your hearts in psalms, hymns, and inspired songs.

IV. Program

The program notes begin on the next page. You are encouraged to build on these ideas. However, each program is self-contained and can be used exactly as is if you desire. Refer to the section entitled "How To Use This Manual" for guidelines on conducting the program.

V. Closing Prayer

Dear Jesus, we are looking forward to the time when we will be healed and renewed, when we will be brought to wholeness in life. Grant us, holy Father, the gift of the inner peace that casts out our inability to forgive and guilt, that allows us to let go of those memories keeping us bound to the past. Amen.

A. Answer the following questions.

1. What have been some of my strongest feelings about the loss of my spouse?

2. Have these feelings changed the way I act toward others or toward myself?

3. What do I need in order to make peace inside myself, with myself?

4. Is there anything that I would like to forgive or be forgiven for today?

B. Break into small groups to discuss the previous questions.

Self-Esteem

How Do You Feel About Responsibility?

I. Opening Prayer

Lord, grant me the strength to take responsibility for my life. Help me to accept the past and not dwell within it. In the future, help me to see your light and to follow in your footsteps, because following in your footsteps will lead me to true happiness and love. Lord, let me not be afraid, for I know that you are with me, and with you by my side, I have nothing to fear. And thank you, Lord, for all your gifts through Christ our Lord. Amen.

II. Business Report

III. Scripture Reading: Matthew 11:28–30

Come to me, all you who are weary and find life burdensome, and I will refresh you. Take my yoke upon your shoulders and learn from me, for I am gentle and humble of heart. Your souls will find rest, for my yoke is easy and my burden light.

IV. Program

The program notes begin on the next page. You are encouraged to build on these ideas. However, each program is self-contained and can be used exactly as is if you desire. Refer to the section entitled "How To Use This Manual" for guidelines on conducting the program.

V. Closing Prayer

Thank you, Lord, for your understanding and acceptance of my past, for the guidance you will bring to my future, and for your unconditional love of me as I am now. Help me to be responsible for my actions so that now my past will fall in your shadow and my future will express your love through me. Help me to accept others now as you have accepted me. Through Christ our Lord. Amen.

A. Read the statements below. In the space provided, write if you agree or disagree and briefly explain why. Can you add any statements to the list?

1. You are responsible for what you say.

2. You are responsible for what you are.

3. You are responsible for what you feel.

4. You are responsible for what you do.

5. You are not responsible for making anyone else happy.

6. You are not responsible for becoming what someone else wants you to be.

7. You are not responsible for distorting the truth to keep from hurting another person's feelings.

8. What can you add?

B. After everyone has finished, break into your small groups to discuss the questions and your replies.

How Do You See Yourself—
A Winner or a Loser?

I. Opening Prayer

Lord, give us a gentle heart, and help us to do loving things to surprise even ourselves. Help us to stop in our daily round of duties, rush, and hurry to smile and to say a brief word to people. Help us to heal what is broken, and to touch with our love that which needs love. Make us more aware of the little surprises that you scatter in our lives like sunshine. Help us to notice the things we have forgotten, and to be grateful for things we may be taking for granted. Lord, as we do the important things in everyday life, help us also to find time for small celebrations. Give us the insight to live each day as if it were a new gift. Through your Spirit, give us a sense of wonder, that we may celebrate all of your gifts to us. Amen.

II. Business Report

III. Scripture Reading: Matthew 6:25–34

I warn you, then: do not worry about your livelihood, what you are to eat or drink or use for clothing. Is not life more than food? Is not the body more valuable than clothes? Look at the birds in the sky. They do not sow or reap, they gather nothing into barns; yet your heavenly Father feeds them. Are not you more important than they? Which of you by worrying can add a moment to his life-span? As for clothes, why be concerned? Learn a lesson from the way the wild flowers grow. They do not work; they do not spin. Yet I assure you, not even Solomon in all his splendor was arrayed like one of these. If God can clothe in such splendor the grass of the field, which blooms today and is thrown on the fire tomorrow, will he not provide much more for you, O weak in faith! Stop worrying, then, over questions like "What are we to eat, or what are we to drink, or what are we to wear?" The unbelievers are always running after these things. Your heavenly Father knows all that you need. Seek first his kingship over you, his way of holiness, and all these things will be given you besides. Enough, then, of worrying about tomorrow. Let tomorrow take care of itself. Today has troubles enough of its own.

IV. Program

The program notes begin on the next page. You are encouraged to build on these ideas. However, each program is self-contained and can be used exactly as is if you desire. Refer to the section entitled "How To Use This Manual" for guidelines on conducting the program.

V. Closing Prayer

Father in heaven, we praise you and honor you because you do all things for our good. When we fall, you pick us up. When we sin, your forgiveness is always available. Teach us, O Lord, not to criticize others or ourselves. Teach us not to judge others or ourselves, because this area belongs to you alone. Teach us instead to love and accept ourselves as we are and to love and accept others as they are, for we are all your creatures. Amen.

A. Go through the following list quickly, rating yourself +1 through +5 for your positive traits and −1 through −5 for your negative traits.

_____ Like myself

_____ Can't hold a job

_____ Afraid of being hurt by others

_____ Trust myself

_____ People can trust me

_____ Usually say the wrong thing

_____ Put up a good front

_____ Enjoy people

_____ Usually say the right thing

_____ Don't like being male/female

_____ Feel bad about myself

_____ Discouraged about life

_____ Fearful of the future

_____ Don't like to be around people

_____ Dependent on others for ideas

_____ Have not developed my talents

_____ Waste time

_____ Glad I'm the sex I am

_____ Use my talents

_____ Often do the wrong thing

_____ Think for myself

_____ Don't understand myself

_____ Help to solve community problems

_____ Know my feelings

_____ Feel hemmed in

_____ People like to be around me

_____ Use time well

_____ Competent on the job

_____ People avoid me

_____ Control myself

_____ Enjoy life

_____ Enjoy work

_____ Trouble controlling myself

_____ Don't enjoy work

_____ Enjoy nature

_____ Don't like myself

_____ Disinterested in community problems

B. Look at the ratings you have given yourself. Is there a pattern? Are they winner traits, loser traits, or a mixture?

C. Answer the following questions.

1. Do the others in the group see you as you see yourself?

2. Are members of the group helpful to you in finding ways to shed loser traits and become a winner?

3. Are you able to help other members of your group do the same?

How Do Others See You?

I. Opening Prayer

Lord, you are so compassionate over all you have created. You are just and forgiving. You sustain us who are wavering in weakness and grant us your grace and strength. You are near enough to hear our every cry, to sense our every need, to grant us whatever is necessary to make us happy and productive as we seek to follow and to serve you. Let us celebrate your eternal mercy and goodness, through Jesus Christ our Lord. Amen.

II. Business Report

III. Scripture Reading: Luke 10:25–37

On one occasion a lawyer stood up to pose him this problem: "Teacher, what must I do to inherit everlasting life?" Jesus answered him: "What is written in the law? How do you read it?" He replied: "You shall love the Lord your God with all your heart, with all your soul, with all your strength, and with all your mind; and your neighbor as yourself." Jesus said, "You have answered correctly. Do this and you shall live." But because he wished to justify himself he said to Jesus, "And who is my neighbor?" Jesus replied: "There was a man going down from Jerusalem to Jericho who fell prey to robbers. They stripped him, beat him, and then went off leaving him half-dead. A priest happened to be going down the same road; he saw him but continued on. Likewise there was a Levite who came the same way; he saw him and went on. But a Samaritan who was journeying along came upon him and was moved to pity at the sight. He approached him and dressed his wounds, pouring in oil and wine. He then hoisted him on his own beast and brought him to an inn, where he cared for him. The next day he took out two silver pieces and gave them to the innkeeper with the request: 'Look after him, and if there is any further expense I will repay you on my way back.' Which of these three, in your opinion, was neighbor to the man who fell in with the robbers?" The answer came, "The one who treated him with compassion." Jesus said to him, "Then go and do the same."

IV. Program

The program notes begin on p. 45. You are encouraged to build on these ideas. However, each program is self-contained and can be used exactly as is if you desire. Refer to the section entitled "How To Use This Manual" for guidelines on conducting the program.

V. Closing Prayer

Forgive me for my unworthy thoughts, O Lord. Overlook my vicious complaints, and so fill my heart with your love that I will respond in love even toward those who cannot love me. Enable me, O Lord, to find my joy in you and to reflect that joy and love to those around me. This I ask in your name. Amen.

A. Circulate among the members of your group, asking them to visualize you as the items listed below. Record several answers for each item.

a color	music
a famous person	a kind of weather
a kind of food	a kind of dog
an article of clothing	a piece of furniture

B. After recording the responses, break into your small groups and discuss the following questions.

1. Do others see you as you see yourself?

2. What messages do you send others to cause them to see you in a particular way?

3. Do you want to send these messages?

4. If you are sending messages other than the ones you want to send, what can you do differently?

Regret

I. Opening Prayer

Lord Jesus, as I look at the past years of my life, the world was mine. There were so many things I had to do, so many things to enjoy, so many goals that were set, so many things to accomplish. As I look back, it seems that I have achieved so little. I have not accomplished all that I wanted to do. But yet, Lord, you were there. You have given me a marvelous gift; you have given me the gift of time. This precious moment I have is mine, and it is really the beginning of the rest of my life. Lord, let me be aware of my place in establishing your kingdom here on earth so that I may contribute. Let me help it be made known to the people who come into my life. Amen.

II. Business Report

III. Scripture Reading: Matthew 16:24–28

Jesus then said to his disciples: "If a man wishes to come after me, he must deny his very self, take up his cross, and begin to follow in my footsteps. Whoever would save his life will lose it, but whoever loses his life for my sake will find it. What profit would a man show if he were to gain the whole world and destroy himself in the process? What can a man offer in exchange for his very self? The Son of Man will come with his Father's glory accompanied by his angels. When he does, he will repay each man according to his conduct. I assure you, among those standing here there are some who will not experience death before they see the Son of Man come in his kingship."

IV. Program

The program notes begin on the next page. You are encouraged to build on these ideas. However, each program is self-contained and can be used exactly as is if you desire. Refer to the section entitled "How To Use This Manual" for guidelines on conducting the program.

V. Closing Prayer

My heart is glad today, O God. I celebrate your presence. I glory in your love for me. I sing your praises. I know to whom I belong and I know where I am going. I know that you are my Lord. I pray, O Lord, that through me you will touch some soul with healing and love. Amen.

A. Read the following quote, and then apply it to a situation in your life. "If I could live my whole life over, this is the one thing I would want most to change."

B. Answer the following questions:

1. Briefly describe the situation you want to change.

2. How do you feel about this situation?

3. What did you want in this situation for yourself? For others?

4. What action did you take at the time?

5. Looking back on this situation now, does it still affect the way you feel about yourself and others?

C. Break into small groups and discuss the questions and your answers.

The Sweat Shirt Game

I. Opening Prayer

Now, O Lord, I have come to a fork in the road. I don't know which way to turn. I commit this day into your hands. I pray that it may be lived by your direction and in accord with your will. I raise my voice in thanksgiving, O God, for you have granted me the assurance that you will guide my faltering steps. Through Christ our Lord. Amen.

II. Business Report

III. Scripture Reading: Luke 18:9–14

He then spoke this parable addressed to those who believed in their own self-righteousness while holding everyone else in contempt: "Two men went up to the temple to pray; one was a Pharisee, the other a tax collector. The Pharisee with head unbowed prayed in this fashion: 'I give you thanks, O God, that I am not like the rest of men—grasping, crooked, adulterous—or even like this tax collector. I fast twice a week. I pay tithes on all I possess.' The other man, however, kept his distance, not even daring to raise his eyes to heaven. All he did was beat his breast and say, 'O God, be merciful to me, a sinner.' Believe me, this man went home from the temple justified but the other did not. For everyone who exalts himself shall be humbled while he who humbles himself shall be exalted."

IV. Program

The program notes begin on the next page. You are encouraged to build on these ideas. However, each program is self-contained and can be used exactly as is if you desire. Refer to the section entitled "How To Use This Manual" for guidelines on conducting the program.

V. Closing Prayer

Break into my darkness, O Lord. Set me free from my troubles. May the daily pressures that threaten me lead me to your grace. Then night will give way to the dawn, depression shall resolve into joy, and I shall sing your praises once more. Through Christ our Lord. Amen.

Many young people happily advertise their feelings, their values, and sometimes their morals by wearing messages printed boldly across their T-shirts or sweat shirts.

Many of us send out strong messages without wearing printed words. (A woman who wears a revealing dress, flutters her eyelashes, and wiggles her hips has on an "I'm available" sweat shirt. People whose shoulders droop, who whine and look anxious, are wearing the message "Pity me" or "Please don't kick me—I'm a victim.")

During this exercise, we are going to remove the "masks" that we wear to hide our inner feelings and let the world know our secret thoughts. We are going to make up our own sweat shirt messages.

What would you like to tell about yourself? BE HONEST!

Examples:

I may not look like much on the outside, but on the inside I'm gorgeous.

I have a lot of love to give, but nobody wants it. Macho Man! . . . I'm really just a teddy bear.

A. TURN THIS PAGE OVER AND WRITE YOUR MESSAGE ON THE BACK. WRITE IT LARGE ENOUGH THAT IT CAN BE READ EASILY.

B. Holding the page against your shirt as though it were written there, circulate among the group for about twenty minutes and discuss the messages. (The group leader should watch the time and announce it to the group.)

C. After everyone is seated, the group leader will ask each person to describe the reactions his message received. Be sure to cover the following information:

Was the message an honest one?

Did you receive positive or negative reactions?

Did those who had cheerful or funny messages receive more attention than the others?

Did anyone feel "put down" by the reactions he or she received?

D. Next, all those in the group should tell what message they wish they could honestly wear. For example: "I'm rich and famous," or "I've got it all together and really don't need this crap," or "I'm the luckiest person on earth."

Self-Esteem

I. Opening Prayer

Dear Lord, give me the strength to love myself as you love me. I will put all thoughts of self-worthlessness behind me. I know that you love me as the unique, special, individual person I am, a person with my own good qualities. By accepting these qualities about myself, I will be able to reach out to others and help them to see these same qualities in them. In reaching out to make my life and the lives of others the very best that they can be, I will be fulfilling your purpose for placing me on earth. Amen.

II. Business Report

III. Scripture Reading: Galatians 6:9–10

Let us not grow weary of doing good; if we do not relax our efforts, in due time we shall reap our harvest. While we have the opportunity, let us do good to all men—but especially those of the household of the faith.

IV. Program

The program notes begin on the next page. You are encouraged to build on these ideas. However, each program is self-contained and can be used exactly as is if you desire. Refer to the section entitled "How To Use This Manual" for guidelines on conducting the program.

V. Closing Prayer

Lord, help me to put all negative thoughts behind me and to dwell on the positive aspects of my life. Give me the strength to learn and grow through my mistakes, to take off my masks and pretenses and be comfortable with being the person I am. Give my life meaning by teaching me to accept the responsibility for my own actions. Through your guidance, help me to create the best life I can possibly have, emotionally, physically and spiritually. Amen.

A. Answer the following questions.

1. What are some of the specific qualities I want others to see in me?

2. What qualities do others see in me? (Based on compliments you receive.)

3. How do I see myself?

4. What do I like about myself?

5. What do I dislike about myself?

6. What specific personal characteristics do I see in myself that make it more difficult for others to love me?

B. Break into small groups to discuss the preceding questions and your answers.

Self-Growth

I. Opening Prayer

God, grant me your wonderful peace that I may experience it in my mind, my soul, and my body. Grant that I keep peace uppermost in my thoughts, and that I feel your peace in my total being. Help me to let go of anxiety and release all tension and fear to you, O Lord. Let me bask in the wonder of your personal presence in and around me. I pray, dear Jesus, that I will hold tightly to love for all, everywhere. Peace and love begin with me, and with your infinite help they will grow. Amen.

II. Business Report

III. Scripture Reading: Mark 6:31–34

He said to them, "Come by yourselves to an out-of-the-way place and rest a little." People were coming and going in great numbers, making it impossible for them to so much as eat. So Jesus and the apostles went off in the boat by themselves to a deserted place. People saw them leaving, and many got to know about it. People from all the towns hastened on foot to the place, arriving ahead of them. Upon disembarking Jesus saw a vast crowd. He pitied them, for they were like sheep without a shepherd; and he began to teach them at great length.

IV. Program

The program notes begin on the next page. You are encouraged to build on these ideas. However, each program is self-contained and can be used exactly as is if you desire. Refer to the section entitled "How To Use This Manual" for guidelines on conducting the program.

V. Closing Prayer

Father in heaven, you have given us a mind to know you, a will to serve you, and a heart to love you. Be with us in all that we do so that your light may shine in our lives. We pray that we may be what you created us to be, and we praise your name in all that we do. Amen.

A. Answer the following questions.

1. In what area of my life am I trying to grow now?

2. How can I benefit from the help of others?

3. How can I continue to learn?

4. How do I feel about being alone?

5. How much time each day (or week) do I think I need to be alone?

6. Do I think that I need more or less time alone than others?

B. Break into small groups to discuss the previous questions and your answers to them.

Resentment

I. Opening Prayer

Lord, help me to let go of the past and stop clinging to old memories. Take away the regrets and failures that have kept me from seeing the wonder and beauty in my life. The hurts of the past are in the past. Help me to leave them there. Through you I can become a new person, meeting life in a new way. Help me see the peace and joy you have sent to fill my life. Through Christ our Lord. Amen.

II. Business Report

III. Scripture Reading: Luke 9:23–27

Jesus said to all: "Whoever wishes to be my follower must deny his very self, take up his cross each day, and follow in my steps. Whoever would save his life will lose it, and whoever loses his life for my sake will save it. What profit does he show who gains the whole world and destroys himself in the process? If a man is ashamed of me and my doctrine, the Son of Man will be ashamed of him when he comes in his glory and that of his Father and his holy angels. I assure you, there are some standing here who will not taste death until they see the reign of God."

IV. Program

The program notes begin on the next page. You are encouraged to build on these ideas. However, each program is self-contained and can be used exactly as is if you desire. Refer to the section entitled "How To Use This Manual" for guidelines on conducting the program.

V. Closing Prayer

O God, how full of wonder and splendor you are. I see the reflections of your beauty and hear the sounds of your majesty wherever I turn. When I gaze into star-studded skies and attempt to comprehend the vast distances, I contemplate in utter amazement my creator's concern for me. I am dumbfounded that you should care personally about me. And yet you made me in your image. You have called me your child. You have ordained me as your priest and chosen me to be your servant. You have assigned to me the fantastic responsibility of carrying on your creative activity. O God, how full of wonder and splendor you are. Amen.

A. Read the following statement, filling in the blank at the end.

I know that the way I grew up had a strong influence on how I perceive myself. The one thing I resent most is:

_____

_____

B. Answer the following questions.

1. How did you feel about the situation you listed above?

2. What did you want in this situation for yourself?

3. What did you want in this situation for others?

4. What action did you take?

5. Looking back on this situation, does it still affect the way you feel about yourself?

6. Looking back on this situation, does it still affect the way you feel about others?

C. Break into small groups to discuss the preceding exercises and your responses to them.

Spiritual Growth

God's Love

I. Opening Prayer

Dear heavenly Father, we thank you for the gift of your Son, our Lord Jesus, and for your Holy Spirit who dwells within us and guides us always. We know of your unconditional love of us and we know of your desire to forgive us, yet we too often find ourselves separated from you. We measure your love by our human standards, so we stay confused. Dear Lord, we pray for your grace. Reveal your love to us and give us the strength to hold fast to you. You made us unique, in your image; now help us to accept what we are. Help us to learn of our gifts from you that make us a part of the body of Christ and a member of the kingdom. Teach us to forgive as you forgive, to accept as you accept, and to love as you love. Amen.

II. Business Report

III. Scripture Reading: John 14:15–21

If you love me and obey the commands I give you, I will ask the Father and he will give you another Paraclete—to be with you always: the Spirit of truth, whom the world cannot accept, since it neither sees him nor recognizes him; but you can recognize him because he remains with you and will be within you. I will not leave you orphaned; I will come back to you. A little while now and the world will see me no more; but you see me as one who has life, and you will have life. On that day you will know that I am in my Father, and you in me, and I in you. He who obeys the commandments he has from me is the man who loves me; and he who loves me will be loved by my Father. I too will love him and reveal myself to him.

IV. Program

The program notes begin on p. 61. You are encouraged to build on these ideas. However, each program is self-contained and can be used exactly as is if you desire. Refer to the section entitled "How To Use This Manual" for guidelines on conducting the program.

V. Closing Prayer

Heavenly Father, we accept your commandments. We know they were given for our benefit—not to make our lives hard, but to draw us closer to you. We accept obedience and submit our wills to you, for you know what is best for us. What we need, you will provide. We place ourselves in your hands, believing that the Holy Spirit dwells in us and answers our prayers. Amen.

A. Read the following quote: "I had decided that God didn't even know my name until he proved his love in a very special way."

B. Think of a time in your life when you could have used the quote to describe your own feelings.

C. Complete the following exercises.

1. Briefly describe the situation that made you feel this way.

2. How did you feel about the situation?

3. What did you want for yourself?

4. What did you want for others?

5. What action did you take?

6. Looking back on this situation now, does it still affect the way you feel about yourself and others? Briefly describe any effects you attribute to this situation.

D. Break into small groups to discuss the previous questions.

Disappointment

I. Opening Prayer

Dear Lord, grant me the strength to live my life completely accepting that which I cannot change. Carry me through the troubled times in my life when I find it hard to walk alone. Make me remember that, with you by my side, I am never alone. Help me to remember your great love for me; give me and all of those who walk with you the gifts of acceptance, courage, joy, and peace. This we ask in your name, through Christ our Lord. Amen.

II. Business Report

III. Scripture Reading: Psalm 31:8–16

I will rejoice and be glad of your kindness, when you have seen my affliction and watched over me in my distress, not shutting me up in the grip of the enemy but enabling me to move about at large. Have pity on me, O Lord, for I am in distress; with sorrow my eye is consumed; my soul also, and my body. For my life is spent with grief and my years with sighing; my strength has failed through affliction, and my bones are consumed. For all my foes I am an object of reproach, a laughingstock to my neighbors, and a dread to my friends; they who see me abroad flee from me. I am forgotten like the unremembered dead; I am like a dish that is broken. I hear the whispers of the crowd, that frighten me from every side, as they consult together against me, plotting to take my life. But my trust is in you, O Lord; I say, "You are my God." In your hands is my destiny; rescue me from the clutches of my enemies and my persecutors.

IV. Program

The program notes begin on the next page. You are encouraged to build on these ideas. However, each program is self-contained and can be used exactly as is if you desire. Refer to the section entitled "How To Use This Manual" for guidelines on conducting the program.

V. Closing Prayer

Lord Jesus Christ, Son of the Father, you became a human person in order to show us how to love. Send us your Spirit so that we may become more aware of the gentle, beautiful things of life. Open our hearts so that we may praise you in these very human things. Amen.

A. Read the following quote; then think back to a time in your life when it described your own feelings. "I really thought I had it all together until this happened."

B. Break into small groups and answer the following questions.

1. Briefly describe the situation that made you feel this way.

2. How did you feel about the situation?

3. What did you want: for yourself? for others?

4. What action did you take?

5. Looking back on this situation now, does it still affect the way you feel about yourself and others?

Christian Living

I. Opening Prayer

Lord, help me to work with you on earth serving others as Christ did. Help me to be worthy of your calling and to live in harmony, peace, and service to others. Help me to expand my spiritual obligations to relationships within your community so that I can enhance the fellowship and overall well-being with your love to all of mankind. This I ask through Christ our Lord. Amen.

II. Business Report

III. Scripture Reading: Colossians 1:9–10

Ever since we heard this we have been praying for you unceasingly and asking that you may attain full knowledge of his will through perfect wisdom and spiritual insight. Then you will lead a life worthy of the Lord and pleasing to him in every way. You will multiply good works of every sort and grow in the knowledge of God.

IV. Program

The program notes begin on the next page. You are encouraged to build on these ideas. However, each program is self-contained and can be used exactly as is if you desire. Refer to the section entitled "How To Use This Manual" for guidelines on conducting the program.

V. Closing Prayer

God, keep me in your service; keep me from looking inward toward myself and keep me looking outward toward others. Keep me loving, kind, unselfish, and at peace. Keep me faithful and patient, not jealous and conceited. Keep me ever mindful of your presence and not absorbed in my pleasures. And, Lord, keep me in your service, not in mine, through Christ our Lord. Amen.

A. Answer the following questions.

1. Serving others is an important element of adult Christian living. How do I think I can best be of service to others?

2. What does it mean to be "holy"? What does it mean to be wholly?

3. Do I think we are called to be "holy"? Wholly?

B. Break into small groups to discuss your answers to the preceding questions.

Love

I. Opening Prayer

Dear Lord, help me to overcome the fears that can isolate me from others. Let me be able to look within myself and see peace, self-understanding, and self-acceptance. Only by doing this will I be able to grow and focus my mind away from my self-centered needs and unconditionally reach out to others with interest, understanding, concern, and acceptance as you do for us. Amen.

II. Business Report

III. Scripture Reading: 1 Corinthians 13:1–2

Now I will show you the way which surpasses all the others. If I speak with human tongues and angelic as well, but do not have love, I am a noisy gong, a clanging cymbal. If I have the gift of prophecy and, with full knowledge, comprehend all mysteries, if I have faith great enough to move mountains, but have not love, I am nothing.

IV. Program

The program notes begin on the next page. You are encouraged to build on these ideas. However, each program is self-contained and can be used exactly as is if you desire. Refer to the section entitled "How To Use This Manual" for guidelines on conducting the program.

V. Closing Prayer

Lord, give me your guidance in experiencing love. We have various types of relationships in our lives, and whatever they may be, let me be thankful for the love I receive from them. Give me the strength to let that love overflow to others, not keep it just for myself. You made us as human beings. Let us accept this and the blessings of life that you gave us, those blessings that enable us to be human, such as caring, hugging, smiling, and loving. Thank you for being a part of our lives. Amen.

A. Answer the following questions.

1. What is my definition of love?

2. Do I see love as a "calling from God"?

3. How does my answer to the last question make me feel?

4. Do I experience God's presence in relationships?

5. How do I experience it?

6. In what sort of situation do I experience it?

7. What are my feelings about God's presence?

B. Break into small groups to discuss the questions and your answers to them.

Talking to God

I. Opening Prayer

Lord, Christ looked up to you for support and strength. Help me to strengthen my faith, Lord; help me to face life's hurts with the courage and ability to move on. So often I have complained about the troubles in my life. I have watched others and asked myself why my life is not as good as theirs. But when I remember Christ's life and his crucifixion, when I recall his strength and faith, I know that, with your help, I will survive. In Christ's name we pray. Amen.

II. Business Report

III. Scripture Reading: Ephesians 3:16–20

And I pray that he will bestow on you gifts in keeping with the riches of his glory. May he strengthen you inwardly through the working of his Spirit. May Christ dwell in your hearts through faith, and may charity be the root and foundation of your life. Thus you will be able to grasp fully, with all the holy ones, the breadth and length and height and depth of Christ's love, and experience this love which surpasses all knowledge, so that you may attain to the fullness of God himself. To him whose power now at work in us can do immeasurably more than we ask or imagine—to him be glory in the church and in Christ Jesus through all generations, world without end. Amen

IV. Program

The program notes begin on the next page. You are encouraged to build on these ideas. However, each program is self-contained and can be used exactly as is if you desire. Refer to the section entitled "How To Use This Manual" for guidelines on conducting the program.

V. Closing Prayer

Dear Lord, there are times when I need someone to talk to. Help me to remember that you are always there and listening. Let me understand your will and follow your guidance. I know that you will always understand and forgive me, but sometimes I need help to understand and forgive myself. Amen.

A. Complete the following exercises.

1. When do you feel most alone? _____

_____

_____

_____

_____

2. Can you talk to God about what is happening in your life? What happens when you do? _____

_____

_____

_____

3. What would you like to say to God tonight? _____

_____

_____

_____

4. If God forgives you, why can't you forgive yourself? _____

_____

_____

_____

_____

_____

B. Break into small groups to discuss the previous questions.

Forgiveness

Forgiveness

I. Opening Prayer

Lord, we ask you to forgive us, and through your love teach us to forgive others. Help us to increase the joy and love so necessary in our lives today so that we may bring more goodness and love to this world. Inspire us with your love so that we will not speak or act in any way that does not show your love and forgiveness. Grant that a spirit of understanding and friendship may prevail in us. Grant us the courage to speak out if anyone is unjustly accused or unfairly treated. And, Lord, we pray that we will always forgive others and live together in happiness and love for all. Amen.

II. Business Report

III. Scripture Reading: John 8:1–11

Jesus went out to the Mount of Olives. At daybreak he reappeared in the temple area; and when the people started coming to him, he sat down and began to teach them. The scribes and the Pharisees led a woman forward who had been caught in adultery. They made her stand there in front of everyone. "Teacher," they said to him, "this woman has been caught in the act of adultery. In the law, Moses ordered such women to be stoned. What do you have to say about the case?" (They were posing this question to trap him, so that they could have something to accuse him of.) Jesus bent down and started tracing on the ground with his finger. When they persisted in their questioning, he straightened up and said to them, "Let the man among you who has no sins be the first to cast a stone at her." A second time he bent down and wrote on the ground. Then the audience drifted away one by one, beginning with the elders. This left him alone with the woman, who continued to stand there before him. Jesus finally straightened up and said to her, "Woman, where did they all disappear to? Has no one condemned you?" "No one, sir," she answered. Jesus said, "Nor do I condemn you. You may go. But from now on, avoid this sin."

IV. Program

The program notes begin on p. 75. You are encouraged to build on these ideas. However, each program is self-contained and can be used exactly as is if you desire. Refer to the section entitled "How To Use This Manual" for guidelines on conducting the program.

V. Closing Prayer

Lord, help me to seek goodness and love in everyone so that I may encourage joy and smiles in their lives. Help me to give my love so that I may reach out to touch everyone in a loving way and hold nothing against them. Let me accept everyone as you have accepted me. You have never ceased to be with me; you have always accepted and loved me. Strengthen this in me so that I may live my life as Christ lived his life for me. Through Christ our Lord. Amen.

A. Answer the following questions.

1. Do I find it easier to forgive friends than enemies?

2. Do I place conditions on my forgiveness?

3. When did I most reach out for someone who hurt me and really forgive that person?

4. When did I most experience God's forgiveness for me?

5. Are there people who still have a hold on my life because I have not forgiven them?

B. Break into small groups to discuss your answers to the previous questions. What did you learn about yourself and your willingness and ability to forgive others? What effect does this have on your life? What can you do about it?

Love Your Enemies

I. Opening Prayer

O Lord Jesus, God of love, you humbled yourself and came to live among us. Let your peace and love be with us. Help us to do your will in all that we say and do. Guide us, Lord, in our grief and worries, our sorrow and pain. Show us your love and give us strength. And above all, Lord, help us to love one another and do your will. We ask this in your name. Amen.

II. Business Report

III. Scripture Reading: John 15:9–17

As the Father has loved me, so I have loved you. Live on in my love. You will live in my love if you keep my commandments, even as I have kept my Father's commandments and live in his love. All this I tell you that my joy may be yours and your joy may be complete. This is my commandment: love one another as I have loved you. There is no greater love than this: to lay down one's life for one's friends. You are my friends if you do what I command you. I no longer speak of you as slaves, for a slave does not know what his master is about. Instead, I call you friends, since I have made known to you all that I heard from my Father. It was not you who chose me, it was I who chose you to go forth and bear fruit. Your fruit must endure, so that all you ask the Father in my name he will give you. The command I give you is this, that you love one another.

IV. Program

The program notes begin on p. 78. You are encouraged to build on these ideas. However, each program is self-contained and can be used exactly as is if you desire. Refer to the section entitled "How To Use This Manual" for guidelines on conducting the program.

V. Closing Prayer

Jesus, you told us to remain in your love and to love our fellow men and to do good to them, no matter who they are or where they are. You know our close friends and you know those who have crossed our paths and no longer are with us. And there are many people, Lord, whom we do not know; yet they are our brothers because of you. We need your help to love all men; teach us how to love them as you love them. Let this love start right here, Lord. Give us patience with one another when things aren't going right. Let us be kind to each other, be honest with each other, and forgive and forget whenever we are hurt. Help us to overcome our anger, our resentments, and our inabilities to cope when things go wrong. There is no limit to your love, Jesus. We beg you to use us so that we can spread your love throughout the world. Amen.

A. Read the following statement; then complete the exercises.

In the Bible, Christ says we should "love our enemies."

1. Briefly explain how you feel about this statement. (Is it easy or difficult? Are you able or not able to do it?)

2. List five ways you are able to show love for an enemy.

3. How did Christ show love for His enemies?

Does Christ's example give you any insight on how to handle painful relationships?

B. Break into small groups to discuss the previous exercises.

"I Wish I Had Said . . ."

I. Opening Prayer

Dear Lord, you know that I still have old hurts and memories that cause me pain. Sometimes they come creeping back in the dark of night, or flash through my mind to put a sudden end to a happy thought. Lord, I need to release myself from these old hurts. Help me to offer them up to you, to cleanse my mind and to open my heart to your inner healing. Through Christ our Lord. Amen.

II. Business Report

III. Scripture Reading: Matthew 25:1–13

The reign of God can be likened to ten bridesmaids who took their torches and went out to welcome the groom. Five of them were foolish, while the other five were sensible. The foolish ones, in taking their torches, brought no oil along, but the sensible ones took flasks of oil as well as their torches. The groom delayed his coming, so they all began to nod, then to fall asleep. At midnight someone shouted, "The groom is here! Come out and greet him!" At the outcry all the virgins woke up and got their torches ready. The foolish ones said to the sensible "Give us some of your oil. Our torches are going out." But the sensible ones replied, "No, there may not be enough for you and us. You had better go to the dealers and buy yourselves some." While they went off to buy it the groom arrived, and the ones who were ready went in to the wedding with him. Then the door was barred. Later the other bridesmaids came back. "Master, master!" they cried. "Open the door for us." But he answered, "I tell you, I do not know you." The moral is: keep your eyes open, for you know not the day or the hour.

IV. Program

The program notes begin on the next page. You are encouraged to build on these ideas. However, each program is self-contained and can be used exactly as is if you desire. Refer to the section entitled "How To Use This Manual" for guidelines on conducting the program.

V. Closing Prayer

God, grant me the serenity to accept the things I cannot change, the courage to change the things I can, and the wisdom to know the difference.—Reinhold Niebuhr (1892–1971)

Many of us have been frustrated at one time or another by not being able to say how we really feel to a former spouse, an employer, a friend, or a child. The reasons are numerous; we fear losing our job, ending a relationship, or hurting someone's feelings.

A. You are now to imagine yourself walking into a soundproof room. The person who hurt you is sitting there, tied to a chair and gagged. You can say anything; the other person cannot interrupt, argue, or respond in any way. Anything you say cannot be held against you, now or in the future.

B. Answer the following questions:

1. Who is in the room?

2. What are you going to say?

C. After everyone has finished, break into your small groups for discussion. During the discussion, answer the following questions:

1. Did it make you feel better to "get it off your chest"?

2. Do you wish you had really said that?

3. Why didn't you? (Fear of reprisal? Fear of causing pain?)

4. Do you think that there is anyone who would like to put you into that soundproof room?

5. Who?

6. What would that person say to you?

7. Would it be right?

Do You Enjoy Hating?

I. Opening Prayer

Lord, help me to forgive the people who hurt me. Sometimes I get so angry when people don't understand me. Don't let this anger separate me from your love. My relationship with you is the most important thing in my life. With your help my life can be beautiful. Don't give up on me, Lord. Help me to forgive others as you always forgive me. Amen.

II. Business Report

III. Scripture Reading: 2 Corinthians 2:10–11

If you forgive a man anything, so do I. Any forgiving I have done has been for your sakes and, before Christ, to prevent Satan—whose guile we know too well—from outwitting us.

IV. Program

The program notes begin on the next page. You are encouraged to build on these ideas. However, each program is self-contained and can be used exactly as is if you desire. Refer to the section entitled "How To Use This Manual" for guidelines on conducting the program.

V. Closing Prayer

Lord, I know there are times when you must really be disappointed in some of the things I say and do. But, with your perfect love, you always forgive me. Help me to develop this kind of love so that I can forgive others in the same way. I know I shouldn't expect others to be perfect when I'm so imperfect. Help me to realize this and to love others the way you love me. This I ask in Christ's name. Amen.

A. Read the following statements.

"Hatred is like fire, it makes even light rubbish deadly."—George Eliot

"Hate is a prolonged form of suicide."—Johan F. von Schiller

"Hate is like a cancer. If you don't get rid of it, it will eat you up."—Clyde Besson

B. Break into small groups. Spend about twenty minutes discussing the statements. Decide if you agree or disagree.

C. Reform the large group and spend about ten minutes disclosing the consensus of the small group to the total assembly.

D. Go back into small groups. Spend about twenty minutes discussing the barriers to forgiveness. Decide how they affect you. The barriers are:

Fear	Humiliation
Pride	Guilt
Unworthiness	Hatred
Bitterness	Resentment

(add others if you think of them)

E. Close the meeting in the large group by summarizing the discussion of barriers. Decide: Is not forgiving or hate worth holding on to and ruining your future happiness in life?

How Can I Learn To Forgive?

I. Opening Prayer

Today, Lord, I pray for forgiveness. I pray that I will forgive those who have brought me sorrow and distress. I pray that I will change that anger to understanding and compassion so that it may help to ease the pain. I know, Lord, that in your love there is forgiveness. I know that, if I cannot forgive, then I cannot love. Grant me the willingness to risk forgiving others so that I can accept your forgiveness of me. Amen.

II. Business Report

III. Scripture Reading: Micah 7:18–19

Who is there like you, the God who removes guilt and pardons sin for the remnant of his inheritance, who does not persist in anger forever, but delights rather in clemency, and will again have compassion on us, treading underfoot our guilt? You will cast into the depths of the sea all our sins.

IV. Program

The program notes begin on the next page. You are encouraged to build on these ideas. However, each program is self-contained and can be used exactly as is if you desire. Refer to the section entitled "How To Use This Manual" for guidelines on conducting the program.

V. Closing Prayer

Lord, it seems as though every time I turn to you, it is to ask for your help. I ask you to take away pain and hurt, to keep me from being disappointed by things that happen in my life, to fulfill my every need. But I don't listen to the things you ask of me. I feel anger, and sometimes even hatred, for others when you have told me so many times to love and forgive. I want to be more like you; I want to do what you ask. Again, I ask for your help. Teach me your perfect love so that I may have the peace that love and forgiveness bring. Amen.

A. Read the following statements; then answer the question.

Forgiveness is painful, illogical, not practical, and is against our human nature.

Forgiveness is embarrassing, often undeserved, and very difficult to do.

In the light of these truths, why does God insist on forgiveness?

B. Think about the following things that God tells us:

Forgive us our trespasses as we forgive others. (Luke 11:3–4)

Father, forgive them, for they know not what they do. (Luke 23:3–4)

Forgive and you will be forgiven. (Colossians 3:13)

Turn the other cheek. (Matthew 5:39)

The Lord does not hold their sin against them. (Acts 7:60)

Happy are the peacemakers. (Matthew 5:9)

C. Discuss how the following elements of the process of forgiveness affect you.
1. The strength to begin forgiving comes from God's grace.
2. You have to want to forgive before you can start forgiving.
3. You must recognize the need within you to forgive.
4. Forgive a little bit at a time until forgiving becomes easier for you.
5. Forgiveness adds to your peace of mind.

Sexuality

NOTE: The next three programs deal with sexual adjustments for the formerly married. There are some definitions concerning sexuality in the beginning of this section. It will be helpful to explain these to your group before getting into the programs.

THREE ASPECTS OF SEXUALITY

(from *Sexual Dimensions of Celibate Life* by Brother James Zullo)

PRIMARY: We are sexually embodied as males and females. We manifest ourselves as masculine and feminine.

GENITAL: Genitality—fantasies, stirrings, desires, urges, physical reactions. Genital behavior—involves sexual arousal and may lead to orgasm.

AFFECTIVE: Feelings, moods, actions that move a person toward another or express closeness. Includes sexual qualities of tenderness, gentleness, and warmth.

DEFINITIONS

(from *The Sexual Celibate* by Donald Goergen)

SEXUALITY: The dimensions of personality that make one male or female, capable of affective bonds and procreative activity, as well as intrinsically structured for an "other." Includes affective, genital, feminine, masculine, heterosexual, homosexual components, achieving its highest manifesting in interpersonal love.

SEXUAL IDENTITY: The psychological process which accompanies puberty and lasts through the 20's. Primarily involves the sense of belonging to one's own sex, as well as an acceptance within oneself of the opposite sex. Also, includes an acceptance of one's sexuality in all its dimensions—an affirmative response to one's sexuality.

AFFECTIVE SEXUALITY: The affectionate, emotional, social, non-procreative dimension of sexuality. Includes sexual qualities of compassion, gentleness, sensitivity, tenderness, and warmth, achieving its highest expression in friendship.

GENITAL SEXUALITY: The biological, physiological, physical, procreative dimension of sexuality. Includes the sexual quality of arousal and achieves its highest expression in orgasm.

SEXUALITY

(from *The Sexual Celibate* by Donald Goergen)

God does not intend us to be alone. Independence is not our goal. Love is the Christian value and sex is a gift from God that exists for the sake of this love. God's intention is not only that two become one but that someday we will all be one as Jesus and his Father are one. Sexuality is a part of the totality of the divine plan. It is not that sexuality is good only in view of reproduction. It is not that the sexual union should be reduced to a minimum in the Christian life. Christians must continue to reflect upon what being sexual means.

Sexual Attitudes

I. Opening Prayer

O Lord, help me to exercise responsibility with the gifts and pleasures you have given me. Help me to be responsible and take into account the other person and perceive how the other person sees our time together. Help me to contribute to others rather than use them; help me always to contribute love to them as you have loved us. This I ask in your name. Amen.

II. Business Report

III. Scripture Reading: 1 John 3:18–20

Little children, let us love in deed and in truth and not merely talk about it. This is our way of knowing we are committed to the truth and are at peace before him no matter what our consciences may charge us with; for God is greater than our hearts and all is known to him.

IV. Program

The program notes begin on the next page. You are encouraged to build on these ideas. However, each program is self-contained and can be used exactly as is if you desire. Refer to the section entitled "How To Use This Manual" for guidelines on conducting the program.

V. Closing Prayer

Lord, I know that I am responsible for my actions and the feelings I have been given. Help me to cope with the problems of single living and to be responsible for my sexuality. Help me to go beyond my own personal gratification and to be enhanced with a love for others, being always mindful of them first in my relationships. Amen.

A. Answer the following questions.

1. In a male/female relationship, sex gets too much attention.

   True   False

2. In a male/female relationship, sex gets too little attention.

   True   False

3. How do you feel about the progression from friendship, to sex, to love, to marriage?

4. What were your strongest negative feelings in your marital sexual relationship?

5. Some formerly married people go into loose sexual patterns trying to resolve other problems such as "Am I still lovable or acceptable?" What are your feelings about this?

B. Break into small groups to discuss the preceding questions and your responses to them.

Single Again—What Is My Attitude About Sex?

I. Opening Prayer

Lord, give me your guidance to resolve the feelings of anxiety, guilt, and denial I experience around sexuality. Give me the strength to dissolve the negative feelings that get in the way of communication and to understand and live in your love. Give me healing and understanding; remove my thoughts of discontent. Give me the knowledge to use your gifts as you intended, ever mindful of others. Through Christ our Lord. Amen.

II. Business Report

III. Scripture Reading: Luke 4:5–8

Then the devil took him up higher and showed him all the kingdoms of the world in a single instant. He said to him, "I will give you all this power and the glory of these kingdoms; the power has been given to me and I give it to whomever I wish. Prostrate yourself in homage before me, and it shall all be yours." In reply, Jesus said to him, "Scripture has it, 'You shall do homage to the Lord your God; him alone shall you adore.' "

IV. Program

The program notes begin on p. 95. You are encouraged to build on these ideas. However, each program is self-contained and can be used exactly as is if you desire. Refer to the section entitled "How To Use This Manual" for guidelines on conducting the program.

V. Closing Prayer

Dear Lord, I know all good things come from you, and when unwanted things confuse me, confound me, and demoralize me, that is when I should call on you to bring good out of my despair. Help me to gain good things from my longings—calm from my anxiety, peace from my anger, and calm assurance over my confusion. Let me know your will, Lord, for I know that your plan for me is better than mine. I have control of my life. I have mastery of my thoughts, my feelings, and my actions. I pray that in all things I may bend my will to yours so that you can complete your perfect work in and through me. Amen.

A. Complete the following exercises.

1. Name some of the prominent sources of your information or education concerning sex and sexuality. (Parents, friends, teachers, church, reading, entertainment, harmful childhood experiences, childhood experiences of love in your home, etc.)

2. Describe your attitudes toward sex and sexuality now. (Confusing, good/bad, mysterious, annoying, frightening, enjoyable, a necessary evil, fearful, necessary, fulfilling, etc.)

3. List the qualities you find desirable and attractive sexually. (Sensitive, tender, physical attributes, vulnerability, need for affection, the need to possess, etc.)

B. Break into small groups to discuss the previous exercise.

Sexual Conduct

I. Opening Prayer

Lord, guide me in my relationships with others. Help me to follow the way of Christ, to go beyond personal gratification to enrichment of your kingdom, to treat others as I want to be treated, to spread your love on earth as Christ did, and to be ever mindful of your presence. I ask this through Christ our Lord. Amen.

II. Business Report

III. Scripture Reading: John 4:8–30, 39–42

His disciples had gone off to the town to buy provisions. The Samaritan woman said to him, "You are a Jew. How can you ask me, a Samaritan and a woman, for a drink?" (Recall that Jews have nothing to do with Samaritans.) Jesus replied: "If only you recognized God's gift, and who it is that is asking you for a drink, you would have asked him instead, and he would have given you living water."

"Sir," she challenged him, "you do not have a bucket and this well is deep. Where do you expect to get this flowing water? Surely you do not pretend to be greater than our ancestor Jacob, who gave us this well and drank from it with his sons and his flocks?" Jesus replied: "Everyone who drinks this water will be thirsty again. But whoever drinks the water I give him will never be thirsty; no, the water I give shall become a fountain within him, leaping up to provide eternal life."

The woman said to him, "Give me this water, sir, so that I shall not grow thirsty and have to keep coming here to draw water."

He said to her, "Go, call your husband, and then come back here." "I have no husband," replied the woman. "You are right in saying you have no husband!" Jesus exclaimed. "The fact is, you have had five, and the man you are living with now is not your husband. What you said is true."

"Sir," answered the woman, "I can see you are a prophet. Our ancestors worshiped on this mountain, but you people claim that Jerusalem is the place where men ought to worship God." Jesus told her: "Believe me, woman, an hour is coming when you will worship the Father neither on this mountain nor in Jerusalem. You people worship what you do not understand, while we understand what we worship; after all, salvation is from the Jews. Yet an hour is coming, and is already here, when authentic worshipers will worship the Father in Spirit and truth. Indeed, it is just such worshipers the Father seeks. God is Spirit, and those who worship him must worship in Spirit and truth."

The woman said to him: "I know there is a Messiah coming. (This term means Anointed.) When he comes, he will tell us everything." Jesus replied, "I who speak to you am he."

His disciples, returning at this point, were surprised that Jesus was speaking with a woman. No one put a question, however, such as "What do you want of him?" or "Why are you talking with her?"

The woman then left her water jar and went off into the town. She said to the people: "Come and see someone who told me everything I ever did! Could this not be the Messiah?" At that they set out from the town to meet him.

Many Samaritans from that town believed in him on the strength of the woman's word of testimony: "He told me everything I ever did." The result was that, when these Samaritans came to him, they begged him to stay with them awhile. So he stayed there two days, and through his own spoken word many more came to faith. As they told the woman: "No longer does our faith depend on your story. We have heard for ourselves, and we know that this really is the Savior of the world."

IV. Program

The program notes begin on the next page. You are encouraged to build on these ideas. However, each program is self-contained and can be used exactly as is if you desire. Refer to the section entitled "How To Use This Manual" for guidelines on conducting the program.

V. Closing Prayer

Lord, I know that I have not always followed your path and I know that you have forgiven me. Help me to do those things in life that please you. Help me to know when I am going astray; help me to go beyond my temptations. Help me to give your love to those around me. Through Christ our Lord. Amen.

A. In the following exercises, circle the answer that best describes how acceptable YOU think the following are in male–female relationships.

	Always	Sometimes	Doubtful	Never
1. holding, hugging	1	2	3	4
2. kissing	1	2	3	4
3. touching, petting	1	2	3	4
4. intimate verbal sharing	1	2	3	4
5. sex with a spouse	1	2	3	4
6. sex with former spouse	1	2	3	4
7. sex in a committed relationship	1	2	3	4
8. sex with a friend	1	2	3	4
9. "one-night stands"	1	2	3	4

B. Circle the answer that best describes how you think others feel.

	Always	Sometimes	Doubtful	Never
1. holding, hugging	1	2	3	4
2. kissing	1	2	3	4
3. touching, petting	1	2	3	4
4. intimate verbal sharing	1	2	3	4
5. sex with a spouse	1	2	3	4
6. sex with former spouse	1	2	3	4
7. sex in a committed relationship	1	2	3	4
8. sex with a friend	1	2	3	4
9. "one-night stands"	1	2	3	4

C. Break into small groups to discuss your answers to the previous exercises.

Trust

Trusting

I. Opening Prayer

O God, sometimes you seem so far away. I cannot sense your presence or feel your power. The darkness about me is stifling; this depression is suffocating. Break into this black night, O God; fill in this vast emptiness. Enter into my conflict lest I fall, never to rise again. I continue to trust in your ever-present love. I shall again discover true joy in my relationship to you. I will proclaim your praises, my Lord, for you will never let me go. Amen.

II. Business Report

III. Scripture Reading: Proverbs 3:5–10

Trust in the Lord with all your heart, on your own intelligence rely not; in all your ways be mindful of him, and he will make straight your paths. Be not wise in your own eyes; fear the Lord and turn away from evil. This will mean health for your flesh and vigor for your bones. Honor the Lord with your wealth, with first fruits of all your produce. Then will your barns be filled with grain, with new wine your vats will overflow.

IV. Program

The program notes begin on the next page. You are encouraged to build on these ideas. However, each program is self-contained and can be used exactly as is if you desire. Refer to the section entitled "How To Use This Manual" for guidelines on conducting the program.

V. Closing Prayer

Please cleanse my mind of past hurts and injustices. Help me to accept others as they are without demanding perfection. Help me to grow in your love and wisdom to become the kind of person I want to be. Let me place my trust in you, Lord, so that I may live with contentment and joy. Amen.

A. Answer the following questions.

1. What are some of your personal fears about building a new relationship?

2. How much does lying affect a relationship?

3. Is there an acceptable degree of lying in a relationship?

4. Describe your reactions to the following statement:

   "Trust is an act of your will."

5. Trust involves trusting yourself, trusting others, and trusting God. What is the common denominator of all three, and why?

B. Break into small groups to discuss the preceding questions and your answers to them.

Being Single

I. Opening Prayer

Lord, sometimes I need people to give me a feeling of being wanted and loved, and sometimes, when people are kind to me, it becomes so easy for me to take advantage of them. I need your guidance, Lord, to be a friend to those who help me. Let me not ask advice, then throw it away. Let me not smother my friends with my self-pity. Help me to be a positive influence on others, forgetting myself and bringing your peace and love into their lives. Amen.

II. Business Report

III. Scripture Reading: Luke 7:44–47

Turning then to the woman, he said to Simon: "You see this woman? I came to your home and you provided me with no water for my feet. She has washed my feet with her tears and wiped them with her hair. You gave me no kiss, but she has not ceased kissing my feet since I entered. You did not anoint my head with oil, but she has anointed my feet with perfume. I tell you, that is why her many sins are forgiven because of her great love. Little is forgiven the one whose love is small."

IV. Program

The program notes begin on the next page. You are encouraged to build on these ideas. However, each program is self-contained and can be used exactly as is if you desire. Refer to the section entitled "How To Use This Manual" for guidelines on conducting the program.

V. Closing Prayer

Thank you, Lord, for all the people who have added so much to my life. Help me always to remember that they are special gifts from you and are to be cherished. Teach me to forget myself and to remember others, to be mindful of their joys and sorrows, to be available when they need me. Most of all, teach me to appreciate their help and understanding. Through Christ our Lord. Amen.

A. Answer the following questions.

1. Name four people you can or do use for support or activities.

2. How would you like to be supported when you are angry? (Be specific about what you want people around you to do.)

3. How would you like to be supported when you are scared? (Be specific about what you want people around you to do.)

4. How would you like to be supported when you are sad? (Be specific about what you want people around you to do.)

5. How would you like to be supported when you are happy? (Be specific about what you want people around you to do.)

B. Break into small groups to discuss the question and your answers to them.

Seeking Support

I. Opening Prayer

Lord, sometimes I feel so alone; it seems as though no one cares about me. Sometimes I need a hand to hold or a shoulder to cry on, but I'm afraid to reach out to someone for help. I don't want to admit my failures, and I'm so afraid of being rejected. Help me to overcome these fears and to accept friendship when it is offered. Let me never forget that you are always with me. Amen.

II. Business Report

III. Scripture Reading: Matthew 25:14–27

The case of a man who was going on a journey is similar. He called in his servants and handed his funds over to them according to each man's abilities. To one he disbursed five thousand silver pieces, to a second two thousand, and to a third a thousand. Then he went away. Immediately the man who received the five thousand went to invest it and made another five. In the same way the man who received the two thousand doubled his figure. The man who received the thousand went off instead and dug a hole in the ground, where he buried his master's money. After a long absence, the master of those servants came home and settled accounts with them. The man who had received the five thousand came forward bringing the additional five. "My lord," he said, "you let me have five thousand. See, I have made five thousand more." His master said to him, "Well done! You are an industrious, reliable servant. Since you were dependable in a small matter I will put you in charge of larger affairs. Come, share your master's joy!" The man who had received the two thousand then stepped forward. "My lord," he said, "you entrusted me with two thousand and I have made two thousand more." His master said to him, "Cleverly done! You too are an industrious and reliable servant. Since you were dependable in a small matter I will put you in charge of larger affairs. Come, share your master's joy!" Finally the man who had received the thousand stepped forward. "My lord," he said, "I knew you were a hard man. You reap where you did not sow and gather where you did not scatter, so out of fear I went off and buried your thousand silver pieces in the ground. Here is your money back." His master exclaimed: "You worthless, lazy lout! You know I reap where I did not sow and gather where I did not scatter. All the more reason to deposit my money with the bankers so that on my return I could have had it back with interest."

IV. Program

The program notes begin on the next page. You are encouraged to build on these ideas. However, each program is self-contained and can be used exactly as is if you desire. Refer to the section entitled "How To Use This Manual" for guidelines on conducting the program.

V. Closing Prayer

Lord, we all know that in a community of brotherhood is the kingdom of God. Therefore, we thank you and give you glory for the friends we have and the new friends you have sent us in our time of need. We give you our everlasting love and devotion, for you know our needs better than we do. We know that you provide for us when we feel alone and lonely and when we feel used or useless. We pray that in your love and understanding you will send us someone who can support us and another who needs our support. This we ask through Christ our Lord. Amen.

A. Complete the following exercises.

1. Describe a specific situation in which you needed a friend.

2. What kind of support did you want at this time? (Listening, stroking, advice, etc.)

3. If you didn't get the support you needed, what did you do?

4. Describe a specific situation when someone needed support from you.

5. How did you react in the above situation?

B. Break into small groups to discuss the previous exercises.

Trust in Self

I. Opening Prayer

Dear God, this is our prayer: that we know your love of us and learn to love ourselves again; that we let go of our fears and let you reveal your peace within us; that we experience your forgiveness and forgive ourselves and others. Amen.

II. Business Report

III. Scripture Reading: Psalm 5:11–12

Punish them, O God; let them fall by their own devices; for their many sins, cast them out because they have rebelled against you. But let all who take refuge in you be glad and exult forever. Protect them, that you may be the joy of those who love your name.

IV. Program

The program notes begin on the next page. You are encouraged to build on these ideas. However, each program is self-contained and can be used exactly as is if you desire. Refer to the section entitled "How To Use This Manual" for guidelines on conducting the program.

V. Closing Prayer

Lord, give me the strength to look deep within myself, the strength to accept who and what I am. Help me to understand myself and others, to accept and trust, to forgive and be forgiven, to love others and to be loved. Let me always remember that life is for trusting, for loving, and for celebrating. Amen.

A. Complete the following exercises.

1. Describe a time when you knew that you lacked trust in yourself.

    a. What caused it?

    b. What outside influences caused you to feel that way?

    c. Have you grown past that stage?

2. What new insights have you discovered?

3. What new inner strengths have surfaced for you?

4. What new opportunities are now open to you?

B. Break into small groups to discuss the previous exercises.

Stages of Trust

I. Opening Prayer

Lord, there are so many decisions to make every day. Help me to choose what is right, not what is easy. Give me the strength to be true to my beliefs without being influenced by others. Help me to move beyond the mistrust and fear that have kept me from living the full, beautiful life that can be mine. Amen.

II. Business Report

III. Scripture Reading: Ephesians 2:8–10

I repeat, it is owing to his favor that salvation is yours through faith. This is not your own doing, it is God's gift; neither is it a reward for anything you have accomplished, so let no one pride himself on it. We are truly his handiwork, created in Christ Jesus to lead the life of good deeds which God prepared for us in advance.

IV. Program

The program notes begin on the next page. You are encouraged to build on these ideas. However, each program is self-contained and can be used exactly as is if you desire. Refer to the section entitled "How To Use This Manual" for guidelines on conducting the program.

V. Closing Prayer

Dear Lord, I get so confused. There are so many people who expect things of me—my family, my friends, my children, the people at work. Sometimes I feel as though I'm being pulled in all directions. When that happens, it's hard to know what is best for me. Please give me peace of mind and let me trust in you to lead me into making the right decisions about my life. Help me to accept myself as I am—your creation. In your love I am complete. Amen.

A. Complete the following exercises.

1. Give your opinion of the following statement: "Each person is as God made him or her. He doesn't make mistakes."

2. If you believe that only you are responsible for what you do, why do you feel guilty when you think you don't measure up to the expectations of:

   a. family?

   b. friends?

   c. church?

   d. society?

   e. others?

3. Do you always make decisions based on what you feel is right or wrong, or do you let others influence you by "ought to, should do, or could do"?

4. Do you always present yourself as the real you or do you put on a mask at times? Which of the following masks do you sometimes wear?

   a. life of the party

   b. super mom or super dad

   c. poor me

   d. got it all together

   e. there's plenty of fish in the sea

   f. I'm finally free

g. no one will ever want me

h. that's the way it goes

i. everybody's doing it

j. I feel like used goods

k. other

5. Under what conditions do you wear a mask, and why?

B. Break into small groups to discuss the previous questions.

Feelings

I. Opening Prayer

Lord, sometimes I really need someone to talk to, but it's so hard to share my feelings with others. I don't want anyone to know that I'm not in control of my life. I don't want to admit that there are problems I can't handle. I feel so alone when there's no one to share my feelings. I know that you are with me, but it would mean so much to have a friend who understands. Please help me to swallow my pride and reach out to others for their love and understanding. Help me to be open to others when they feel as I do now. Amen.

II. Business Report

III. Scripture Reading: John 15:13–17

There is no greater love than this: to lay down one's life for one's friends. You are my friends if you do what I command you. I no longer speak of you as slaves, for a slave does not know what his master is about. Instead, I call you friends, since I have made known to you all that I heard from my Father. It was not you who chose me, it was I who chose you to go forth and bear fruit. Your fruit must endure, so that all you ask the Father in my name he will give you.

IV. Program

The program notes begin on the next page. You are encouraged to build on these ideas. However, each program is self-contained and can be used exactly as is if you desire. Refer to the section entitled "How To Use This Manual" for guidelines on conducting the program.

V. Closing Prayer

Dear Lord, thank you for sending me good friends who care about me and understand when things aren't going the way I think they should. Thank you for their kindness and love, for the laughter we share during the good times and the tears we share during bad times. Stay near me always, Lord. With your help and the help of the friends you have given me, I will be able to handle anything. Amen.

A. Answer the following questions.

1. How do you feel about sharing your feelings with others?

2. Do you actually share your feelings with someone? Who is it?

3. What do you find difficult about sharing feelings?

4. Do you find some feelings more difficult to share than others? Which ones?

5. Do you believe that sharing your feelings with someone would help you have a closer friendship?

6. Is there someone with whom you would like to share more of your feelings when you leave here? Who is it? What do you want to say to this person?

B. Think about the following statements. Discuss them in groups if there is time.

Feelings are always first person singular.

Feelings are not right or wrong, good or bad, moral or immoral.

Feelings are an inner response. They come spontaneously.

We have feelings whether we want them or not.

We cannot control our feelings, but we can control the way we express them and what we do about them.

When you share a feeling, it is helpful to tell the story that goes with it.

Sometimes I Need a Friend

I. Opening Prayer

Holy Father, we thank you for your everlasting friendship, your unrestricted love, and your constant guidance. We pray for your help in establishing new relationships and new friends. We pray that you will give us courage to step out and not be afraid of meeting and loving new friends. We ask your guidance in accepting and not judging other people, and we pray that you will heal us so that we can be available to be friends toward others. We ask all of these things in the name of Jesus Christ, your Son our Lord. Amen.

II. Business Report

III. Scripture Reading: John 13:34–35

I give you a new commandment: Love one another. Such as my love has been for you, so must your love be for each other. This is how all will know you for my disciples: by your love for one another.

IV. Program

The program notes begin on the next page. You are encouraged to build on these ideas. However, each program is self-contained and can be used exactly as is if you desire. Refer to the section entitled "How To Use This Manual" for guidelines on conducting the program.

V. Closing Prayer

Dear Lord, please keep me reminded that the world doesn't revolve around me. Teach me to put my troubles aside and find joy in helping others. Help me to cherish the friends you have given me and to be open to them when they need a helping hand or a shoulder to cry on. I know you are my strength, my comfort and joy. Amen.

A. Read the following scenario.

Things have not been going well and you really feel the need to talk to a friend. You pick up the phone and call, then end up listening to all your friend's problems. When you hang up an hour later, you still haven't had a chance to mention your troubles.

B. Answer the following questions.

1. Has anything similar ever happened to you? What?

2. How did you feel?

3. Would you choose this person to call again when you need support? Why or why not?

C. Read the following scenario.

You've had a terrible week. Everything that could go wrong did. You're ready to blow your stack. Although you'd really like to talk about it, you don't want to burden anyone with your problems. The phone rings and you hear a friend's voice. It's like a gift from heaven. You unload your troubles and feel like a new person.

D. Answer the following questions.

1. Has anything similar ever happened to you? What?

2. How did you feel?

3. Would you choose this person to call if you again need support? Why or why not?

E. Break into small groups to discuss the previous questions.

Parenting

Parenting

I. Opening Prayer

Lord, I come to you in my confusion and doubt, asking for your strength and wisdom. You know that I want what is best for my children, but sometimes I'm not sure what is best for them. It's so easy to give too little or too much. Give me the time and understanding I need to be the kind of parent you want me to be. Let my home be a place of your love and peace. Through Christ our Lord. Amen.

II. Business Report

III. Scripture Reading: Luke 9:46–48

A discussion arose among them as to which of them was the greatest. Jesus, who knew their thoughts, took a little child and placed it beside him, after which he said to them, "Whoever receives this child in my name receives me, and whoever welcomes me welcomes him who sent me, for the least one among you is the greatest."

IV. Program

The program notes begin on the next page. You are encouraged to build on these ideas. However, each program is self-contained and can be used exactly as is if you desire. Refer to the section entitled "How To Use This Manual" for guidelines on conducting the program.

V. Closing Prayer

Loving Father of us all, give us patience today with those who annoy us, sympathy for those in trouble, and the love that reflects your loving forgiveness for all mankind. Help us to listen to other people in the spirit of your love. Inspire us to value even the small things of life and to meet the great things with generous courage. May your grace inspire all our actions and sustain them to the end so that all our prayer and work may begin in you and by you be completed. Through Christ our Lord. Amen.

A. Study the following situations and answer the given questions.

1. Your best friend has lost his (or her) spouse and has come to you for advice on how to handle his (or her) children. What do you tell him (or her)?

2. Look back over your life since you lost your spouse. Is there any situation with your children that you wish you had handled differently?

3. Are you able to put aside your feelings about your former spouse in order to make the situation easier for your children? Do you find this difficult to do?

4. Your marriage ended in divorce. While talking with your children, it becomes clear that they do not see marriage as "until death do us part." Do you attempt to change their thinking? What do you say?

B. Break into small groups to discuss your answers to the previous questions. Do you have anything to add?

Single Parenting

I. Opening Prayer

We thank you, Lord, for the care and the love you have shown us. Forgive us each time we fail to care for and love those around us. We thank you for your patient mercy with our faults and failings and for the strength you give us to overcome difficulties. Look after all the members of our families. Watch over them in everything they do each day. And bring us closer together in your love. Amen.

II. Business Report

III. Scripture Reading: Matthew 19:13–15

At one point children were brought to him so that he could place his hands on them in prayer. The disciples began to scold them, but Jesus said, "Let the children come to me. Do not hinder them. The kingdom of God belongs to such as these." And he laid his hands on their heads before he left that place.

IV. Program

The program notes begin on the next page. You are encouraged to build on these ideas. However, each program is self-contained and can be used exactly as is if you desire. Refer to the section entitled "How To Use This Manual" for guidelines on conducting the program.

V. Closing Prayer

We thank you, Father, for the joy that children bring us. In them life is fresh and full of promise; may we learn from them innocence and trust. Lead our families to live in harmony. Where there has been anger and hurt, let them be forgotten and new understanding be found. Help us to live in love through your grace. Amen.

A. Answer the following set of questions appropriate to your status.

(FOR THE SEPARATED AND DIVORCED)

1. How do your children relate to the absentee parent?

2. What picture of your former spouse do you present to your children?

3. How did you tell your children about your divorce?

4. How did your children react when you told them about the divorce?

5. If problems arise, where can you seek help?

(FOR THE WIDOWED)

1. How have your children adjusted to the loss of their other parent?

2. What picture of your former spouse do you present to your children?

3. How did your child react to the death of this parent?

4. How did you deal with that reaction?

5. If problems arise where can you seek help?

B. Break into small groups to discuss the above questions and your answers to them.

Thoughts on Single Parenting

I. Opening Prayer

O God, the obstacles that confront me today are so many. Even as they press in on me, there are people around me who laugh at my childlike dependence on you. They claim that my faith is futile, that God is not interested in my petty problems. But yet I constantly seek your deliverance from all that hurts or hinders. You are able to rid my life of everything that may threaten my relationship with you. You will, in your own good time, set me free from every human fault and frailty. But even while I seek your ultimate deliverance, help me to sense your presence and power in the midst of my many conflicts. Amen.

II. Business Report

III. Scripture Reading: Mark 10:13–16

People were bringing their little children to him to have him touch them, but the disciples were scolding them for this. Jesus became indignant when he noticed it and said to them: "Let the children come to me and do not hinder them. It is to just such as these that the kingdom of God belongs. I assure you that whoever does not accept the reign of God like a little child shall not take part in it." Then he embraced them and blessed them, placing his hands on them.

IV. Program

The program notes begin on the next page. You are encouraged to build on these ideas. However, each program is self-contained and can be used exactly as is if you desire. Refer to the section entitled "How To Use This Manual" for guidelines on conducting the program.

V. Closing Prayer

Dear God, give me the courage and strength I need to walk this road I've found myself upon—the road trying to raise children on my own. Give me the knowledge, love, and patience to give my children a warm, loving home. Help me not to instill in my children a bitterness or resentment toward others and to help them understand that God does love them regardless of what has happened to us. Most of all, God, give me the strength to look to the future and not the past. Please take away this hurt in my heart and help me to come out of this experience a whole person, better for having gone through it. Amen.

A. Answer the following questions.

1. When are you totally honest with your children? When not? (Santa, the stork, the tooth fairy, etc.)

2. What is your justification for the answer you gave to the last question?

3. What are the subjects you find difficult to discuss with your children?

4. How do you feel about being both parents to your child? And how do you cope with it?

5. At what age do you feel that your responsibility to your children ends? Why?

B. Break into small groups to discuss the previous questions and your answers to them.

Single Parenting Problems

I. Opening Prayer

Dear Lord, please help me through the times when I'm having difficulties with my children, when I feel all alone and that I have no one to turn to. Help me to understand why we are responding to each other as we are. Give me the strength and patience to turn to my friends for support and to you for wisdom. We are all your children and we trust in your guidance. Amen.

II. Business Report

III. Scripture Reading: Ephesians 6:5–8

Slaves, obey your human masters with the reverence, the awe, and the sincerity you owe to Christ. Do not render service for appearance only and to please men, but do God's will with your whole heart as slaves of Christ. Give your service willingly, doing it for the Lord rather than men. You know that each one, whether slave or free, will be repaid by the Lord for whatever good he does.

IV. Program

The program notes begin on the next page. You are encouraged to build on these ideas. However, each program is self-contained and can be used exactly as is if you desire. Refer to the section entitled "How To Use This Manual" for guidelines on conducting the program.

V. Closing Prayer

Dear Father in heaven, I need you. I need to trust in your wisdom and your strength so that I can raise my children, your gifts, in accordance with your desires. Mother Mary, pray for me so that I will be able to raise my children as you raised your Son, Jesus Christ. Father, I pray that my children will accept me and help me hold together this family. Amen.

A. Complete the following exercises.

1. Do you have any guilt feelings about being a single parent? Identify and explain.

2. How did you adjust the time spent with your children after you became a single parent?

3. What are the biggest problem areas you have about single parenting?

4. What are the biggest problem areas your children have about single parenting?

5. What are your ideas about:

    a. normal family?

    b. broken home?

    c. father image?

    d. mother image?

B. Break into small groups to discuss the previous questions.

Special Problems

How Would You Handle This?

I. Opening Prayer

Dear Father, we always put our trust in you. We ask in return that you strengthen our ability to trust others. It is so very rewarding when we can accept others just as they are or where they are. Too often we fall short. By judging others we pass up so many opportunities for new and valuable friends. Teach us your mercy for all. We pray for compassion to others and for ourselves so that we can grow and become more like you. Amen.

II. Business Report

III. Scripture Reading: Romans 12:9–17

Your love must be sincere. Detest what is evil, cling to what is good. Love one another with the affection of brothers. Anticipate each other in showing respect. Do not grow slack but be fervent in spirit; he whom you serve is the Lord. Rejoice in hope, be patient under trial, persevere in prayer. Look on the needs of the saints as your own; be generous in offering hospitality. Bless your persecutors; bless and do not curse them. Rejoice with those who rejoice, weep with those who weep. Have the same attitude toward all. Put away ambitious thoughts and associate with those who are lowly. Do not be wise in your own estimation. Never repay injury with injury. See that your conduct is honorable in the eyes of all.

IV. Program

The program notes begin on the next page. You are encouraged to build on these ideas. However, each program is self-contained and can be used exactly as is if you desire. Refer to the section entitled "How To Use This Manual" for guidelines on conducting the program.

V. Closing Prayer

Heavenly Father, you are always present when we are in need; you know all things, even our deepest thoughts; in your power you can inspire us to a better life. We ask in humility for guidance and charity to overcome our inconsistencies and failures. We pray to be more like you in forgiveness, charity, and good fellowship. Amen.

A. Read the following story.

A new person comes to your support-group meeting. She is brought by a friend and obviously doesn't feel that she is in the "same boat" with everyone else. Her marriage ended six months ago, and she feels that she has it all together. However, she withdraws when the hugging starts and is particularly distant with the men in the group. During a discussion period, it becomes apparent that she is stuck in the anger stage of the grieving process.

B. Use the following exercises to describe the ways in which you would help this person to grow, other than recommending counseling. Would you:

1. confront her anger in front of the group?

2. talk to her friend and find out more about her, making sure she really is stuck in the anger stage?

3. talk to her personally after the meeting?

4. call her later in the week after the meeting and discuss her reaction to the support group, talk her into coming to the next meeting, overcome her objections, and pick her up if necessary?

5. put the meeting agenda aside and suggest a short discussion on anger or the five stages of grief?

6. talk to the program chairman and see if he can schedule a program on anger or the five stages of grief in the near future?

7. just hope she keeps coming back until she works it out?

C. Break into small groups to discuss the responses to the previous exercises.

Where Do I Fit In?

I. Opening Prayer

Lord, help us to reach out with open hearts to those who are hurting. Help us to hear what isn't said in words. Teach us not to judge others but to love them. Be with us every time we meet; use each one of us as an instrument of your peace and love. Amen.

II. Business Report

III. Scripture Reading: Romans 9:28–31

For quickly and decisively will the Lord execute sentence upon the earth. It is just as Isaiah predicted: "Unless the Lord of hosts had left us a remnant, we should have become like Sodom, we should be like Gomorrah." How, then, shall we put it? That the Gentiles, who were not seeking justice, attained it—the justice which comes from faith—while Israel, seeking a law from which justice would come, did not arrive at that law?

IV. Program

The program notes begin on the next page. You are encouraged to build on these ideas. However, each program is self-contained and can be used exactly as is if you desire. Refer to the section entitled "How To Use This Manual" for guidelines on conducting the program.

Note to the Group Leader: When the discussion starts, pay particular attention to the answers given to question 5. Are your group members judging the person's feelings? If so, gently bring it to their attention and remind them that feelings are not right or wrong; they just are.

V. Closing Prayer

Lord, help us not to pass judgment on one another but rather to understand and love. Give us patience without complaint, trust without suspicion, and regard for others rather than for ourselves. Take away our anger and our distress and give us faith, hope, and affection. This we ask through Christ our Lord. Amen.

A. Read the following story.

Your marriage has ended. It's been months and you keep thinking that things should be better, but no matter what you do, the hurt just won't go away. A friend tells you about a support group where people who are hurting get together and give each other emotional support. It sounds like just what you've been looking for.

You go to the meeting and hear a report from the social chairman on an upcoming dance. The publicity chairman hands out a calendar of social events and activities for the month. The program for the meeting is on sexuality and the hand-out contains words you find crude and unacceptable for mixed company. Totally disheartened, you can't wait for the meeting to be over, and you vow never to come back.

B. Complete the following exercises.

1. Do you think that the person's expectations were unrealistic?

2. Do you think that the person just wasn't ready for a support group?

3. Could this situation happen at your support group?

4. How does your support group ensure that something similar to this situation won't happen?

5. What did you think of the person in the story?

6. Did you think that the person was justified in his feelings?

7. Why did you give the answer that you gave to the last question?

C. Break into small groups to discuss the responses to the previous exercises.

With Friends Like This . . .

I. Opening Prayer

Dear God, there are times when my jealousy and anger at others' happiness is almost more than I can bear. Please help me to recognize, understand, and accept these feelings when they creep into my life. Help me to let them go before they do harm to others and to me. With you beside me giving me strength, I can increase my feelings of self-worth and accept people as they are. Amen.

II. Business Report

III. Scripture Reading: Mark 2:24–26

At this the Pharisees protested: "Look! Why do they do a thing not permitted on the sabbath?" He said to them: "Have you never read what David did when he was in need and he and his men were hungry? How he entered God's house in the days of Abiathar the high priest and ate the holy bread which only the priests were permitted to eat? He even gave it to his men."

IV. Program

The program notes begin on the next page. You are encouraged to build on these ideas. However, each program is self-contained and can be used exactly as is if you desire. Refer to the section entitled "How To Use This Manual" for guidelines on conducting the program.

V. Closing Prayer

Lord, yesterday I asked for your forgiveness, and today I didn't forgive. I asked for your love, and today I didn't love. I asked for your help, and today I wasn't helpful. I asked you to be patient with me, and today I was abrupt with another. Now, Lord, I ask for your guidance so that I might give to others what you have given me. Amen.

A. Read the following story.

Joan is finally starting to recover. The anger and hurt aren't so strong anymore, but learning to trust is going to take a lot longer. Feelings of failure are still keeping her self-esteem at a low level and she can't really see herself ever romantically involved again. Recently Joan has been working in close proximity with a new employee. This girl has been married less than two years, and her every sentence begins, "My husband . . . " She's a very nice person and obviously very much in love with her husband. However, by the end of the second week, Joan is ready to throw up every time the girl opens her mouth.

B. Complete the following exercises.

1. Is it possible that Joan is transferring old anger that she felt toward her former spouse to the new girl at work?

2. Is it possible that Joan is jealous of the relationship between the new girl and her husband?

3. Is it possible that the stories that the new girl keeps telling are stirring up too many old memories for Joan?

4. How do you feel about the new girl? Do you think that she is totally insensitive?

5. How do you feel about Joan? Do you think that she is totally insensitive?

6. How should Joan handle the situation?

C. Break into small groups to discuss the previous exercises.

Tomorrow

I. Opening Prayer

Lord, thank you for the friends who overlook my faults and love me for myself, for those who see what I can be, for those who, in their way, add so much pleasure to my life. Thank you for those who see my needs and reach out a hand to help, for those who pray for me, for the ones who understand me and are always there. Lord, bless all these friends who accept me, help me smile, and walk with me from day to day. For this I pray. Amen.

II. Business Report

III. Scripture Reading: Psalm 34:7–11

When the afflicted man called out, the Lord heard, and from all his distress he saved him. The angel of the Lord encamps around those who fear him, and delivers them. Taste and see how good the Lord is; happy the man who takes refuge in him. Fear the Lord, you holy ones, for naught is lacking to those who fear him. The great grow poor and hungry; but those who seek the Lord want for no good thing.

IV. Program

The program notes begin on the next page. You are encouraged to build on these ideas. However, each program is self-contained and can be used exactly as is if you desire. Refer to the section entitled "How To Use This Manual" for guidelines on conducting the program.

V. Closing Prayer

Lord, help me to feed the hungry minds with your words. Help me to fill the thirsty mouths with a cup of your love. Lead me to the sick in heart and those imprisoned in depression. Let me clothe the naked soul, shelter the loneliness of others, and receive the stranger in his or her hour of darkness. This I ask in Christ our Lord. Amen.

A. Complete the following exercises.

1. One thing that I would like to change in my family is:

2. One thing that I would like to change about my work is:

3. One thing that I would like to change in my friendships is:

4. One way that I can make my life happier is:

5. One way that I would like to get closer to God is:

6. The kind of person that I would like to be in five years is:

7. To begin to be that kind of person now, I can:

8. I feel uptight or uncomfortable about (choose three and tell why):

   a. relationships   b. my job
   c. disciplining my children   d. being a single person
   e. being a single parent   f. my former spouse
   g. my family   h. something not listed

9. When someone close to me is hostile or unhappy, I usually (choose one or more and explain):

a. want to get away from them b. feel helpless
c. want to make them feel better d. wish I had helped
e. cry f. swear
g. feel like or react by
(something not listed)

10. How can you change the way you usually act?

11. The special thing about my family is:

B. Break into small groups to discuss the previous questions.

Values

Lost in a Lifeboat

I. Opening Prayer

Dear Father, we know that you promised us that when two or more are gathered together in your name, you are with us. We accept this promise and thank you for it. We thank you for all the blessings you have given us—our talents, our abilities, and our freedom to choose. Often, dear God, we choose to do wrong, and we ask your forgiveness for those times. It is our faith that you will supply all our needs and use all occasions to draw us back to you to live our lives in your kingdom. Jesus, we believe; please pray for our unbelief. Amen.

II. Business Report

III. Scripture Reading: Matthew 26:47–52

While he was still speaking, Judas, one of the twelve, arrived accompanied by a great crowd with swords and clubs. They had been sent by the chief priests and elders of the people. His betrayer had arranged to give them a signal, saying, "The man I shall embrace is the one; take hold of him." He immediately went over to Jesus, said to him, "Peace, Rabbi," and embraced him. Jesus answered, "Friend, do what you are here for!" At that moment they stepped forward to lay hands on Jesus, and arrested him. Suddenly one of those who accompanied Jesus put his hand to his sword, drew it, and slashed at the high priest's servant, cutting off his ear. Jesus said to him: "Put back your sword where it belongs. Those who use the sword are sooner or later destroyed by it."

IV. Program

The program notes begin on p. 145. You are encouraged to build on these ideas. However, each program is self-contained and can be used exactly as is if you desire. Refer to the section entitled "How To Use This Manual" for guidelines on conducting the program.

V. Closing Prayer

Almighty God, you have forgiven me so many times for my trespasses against your will that I cannot count them. You have listened patiently to my complaining and consoled me in times of hardship. Let me remember your unfathomable love for me when I am called upon to deal with compassion toward some other person. I often have less patience with other people than I should. You have shown me how to act, what to say, and what to do; yet I continue to ignore the example of Christ and sometimes react without forgiveness for others. Grant that I may recognize this failing in myself and remember the teaching of Christ the next time I encounter such a situation. Amen.

A. Read the following story. (This exercise will help to show you how your personal values affect your decision making.)

Pretend that you are aboard a luxury liner in the middle of the Pacific Ocean. Dusk is approaching when you hear the alert signal to abandon ship. Passengers pour into the lifeboats. Suddenly a bomb explodes, destroying everything on the ship and killing hundreds of passengers who did not have time to get into a lifeboat. What is left of the ship sinks. You are in a lifeboat built to carry eight people; it is now holding fifteen. There is only enough water to supply ten people for three days. Even with these negative points, you decide to try saving all fifteen people. However, to plan ahead, you think that the group should rank the people, deciding who is to go and who is to stay.

First, rank the people yourself. Use a scale of 1 to 15, with 1 being the most necessary person to stay and 15 being the first to go. Use the information from the story and that provided in the following list to perform the ranking. Next, rank the people with your group. The column marked YD is for your decision; the column marked GD is for the group's decision.

		YD	GD
1.	Minister, 25, single, male		
2.	Electrical engineer, 45, female		
3.	Olympic swimmer, 40, male		
4.	Doctor, 35, married, 3 children at home, female		
5.	Artist, 60, widowed, male		
6.	Navy captain, retired, 70, divorced, male		
7.	Nurse, 30, married, no children, female		
8.	Pregnant lady, 27, unmarried		
9.	Boy, 14, epileptic		
10.	Rabbi, 40, male		
11.	Campus militant, 21, female		
12.	Scientist, 36, married, 2 children, can't swim		

13. Boy, 7, only child

14. Housewife, 45, married, 2 children, can't swim

15. Ex-con (armed robbery), 31, single, 2 children, male

C. Discuss the following questions.

1. On what values did you base your decisions?

2. On what values did your group base its decisions?

3. Did your values remain the same throughout or did they change under peer pressure?

Complete the Thought

I. Opening Prayer

Dear Lord, please give me the strength to understand and accept myself and others as you have made us. We are all your children. Please let us see the things we sometimes miss because our eyes are so limited and focused on ourselves. Give us your vision, your strength, and your love. Amen.

II. Business Report

III. Scripture Reading: John 14:5–9

"Lord," said Thomas, "we do not know where you are going. How can we know the way?" Jesus told him: "I am the way, and the truth, and the life; no one comes to the Father but through me. If you really knew me, you would know my Father also. From this point on you know him; you have seen him." "Lord," Philip said to him, "show us the Father and that will be enough for us." "Philip," Jesus replied, "after I have been with you all this time, you still do not know me? Whoever has seen me has seen the Father. How can you say, 'Show us the Father'?"

IV. Program

The program notes begin on p. 149. You are encouraged to build on these ideas. However, each program is self-contained and can be used exactly as is if you desire. Refer to the section entitled "How To Use This Manual" for guidelines on conducting the program.

NOTE TO PROGRAM LEADER: You can use this program in two ways.

1. You can have the group form a circle, then read the first part of each sentence. Let each member of the group give a response.

2. Copy the program page, distribute it to each member to fill out, then discuss the answers.

V. Closing Prayer

Dear Lord, you have given me a beautiful world to live in and so many good people to share it. Help me to see everything as your creation and to see you in everyone I meet. Give me the strength to reject those things of the world that separate us and draw near those things that bring us closer together. Give me the courage to live by my beliefs, the compassion to reach out to others who need understanding, and the awareness that my life is a gift from you. Amen.

A. Complete the following sentences. (This exercise in free association will help you to know yourself and others better.)

1. On Saturday nights, I like most to

2. When it rains, I

3. In my spare time, I

4. Abortion is

5. Women's lib really

6. Sex before marriage

7. As a social institution, marriage

8. I think homosexuals

9. I think that marijuana

10. I cry when

11. I feel most comfortable in a small group when

12. People bother me when

13. _____ makes me feel very self-conscious.

14. I get ticked off

15. Religion is something

16. The out-of-doors makes me feel

17. The mountains make me aware

18. If I had six months to live, I would

19. My mother

20. My father

21. If I could change one thing about myself, I would

22. The thing I like most about myself is

23. I feel very inferior when

24. The situation I feel most secure in is

25. Of all the many faces of myself, I like the role of

26. Game-playing is something that

27. Most of all, I want to

28. Intellectually, I

29. I make myself laugh when I

B. Discuss the following questions.

1. What, if anything, did you learn about yourself?

2. What, if anything, did you learn about the others in your group?

3. Were you surprised by any of the responses given by others?

4. Did you discover any misconceptions you may have had about any member of your group or yourself?

The Nuclear War

I. Opening Prayer

Lord, you are my constant companion. There is no need that you cannot fulfill. Whether your course for me points to the mountaintops of glorious ecstasy or to the valleys of human despair I know you are at my side. You are ever present with me. You are close beside me when I tread the dark streets of danger. Even when I flirt with death itself, you will not leave me. When the pain is severe, you are near to comfort; when the burden is heavy, you are there to lean upon; when depression darkens my soul, you fill the aching vacuum with your power. My security is in your promise to be near to me always, and in the knowledge that you will never let me go. Amen.

II. Business Report

III. Scripture Reading: Matthew 24:4–14

In reply Jesus said to them: "Be on guard! Let no one mislead you. Many will come attempting to impersonate me. 'I am the Messiah!' they will claim, and they will deceive many. You will hear of wars and rumors of wars. Do not be alarmed. Such things are bound to happen, but that is not yet the end. Nation will rise against nation, one kingdom against another. There will be famine and pestilence and earthquakes in many places. These are the early stages of the birth pangs. They will hand you over to torture and kill you. Indeed, you will be hated by all nations on my account. Many will falter in betraying and hating one another. False prophets will rise in great numbers to mislead many. Because of the increase of evil, the love of most will grow cold. The man who holds out to the end, however, is the one who will see salvation. This good news of the kingdom will be proclaimed throughout the world as a witness to all the nations. Only after that will the end come."

IV. Program

The program notes begin on p. 153. You are encouraged to build on these ideas. However, each program is self-contained and can be used exactly as is if you desire. Refer to the section entitled "How To Use This Manual" for guidelines on conducting the program.

V. Closing Prayer

Grant me, O God, a measure of ecstasy. Help me to feel good about myself and about my role in your service. Reveal yourself in some special way that I may rest in joy and in peace. Through Christ our Lord. Amen.

A. Break into small groups and read the following story, pretending that it is true. (This exercise will help to show you how prejudices, values, and personal needs influence decisions.)

The United States has been involved in a nuclear war. Ten people find themselves in a shelter capable of supporting only five people for the year of necessary confinement. There are no other shelters known to have survived the attack. Your group must evict five people so that the remaining five may survive.

B. First, study the ten short biographies of the people in your shelter. Then, with your group, decide whom to evict. On the biography sheet, place a plus mark (+) beside the names of those individuals that your group decides can stay in the shelter. Place a minus mark (−) beside the names of those your group decides to evict.

C. Reassemble into the large group for discussion. Answer the following questions:

1. How do the groups differ in their decisions?

2. Do individual prejudices really affect values and decision making?

3. If you think that prejudice affects values and decision making, explain how.

4. Is gender, age, or race a contributing factor in making decisions?

5. By what criteria were your judgments made? (Who could best help the group? Who deserved to live?)

6. Did you have to compromise within your group?

7. If you had to compromise, was it easy or difficult?

PERSONALITIES

ALICE   Is a brilliant science professor. She teaches and is doing cancer research. Although she is cold and impersonal, the group has already recognized her as a good organizer and pacifier.

SALLY   Is a nurse. Extremely intelligent, she first completed nurse's training, then received a degree allowing her to teach training courses for nurses. Very fastidious, she is offended by the idea of no bath, wearing the same clothes for a month, and sleeping with other people.

LINDA   Is a literature major. She has read extensively, traveled widely, and had many interesting experiences that she can share. She has published several short stories, is a good story teller and has entertained the group with some of her stories. She is a former member of the peace corps and has had survival training.

FRED   Is a medical student. He completed two years of medical school and four years as a navy medical assistant. He is close to his father, a doctor. He would undoubtedly be a great asset to the group, but refuses to stay unless his wife also stays.

DONNA   Is Fred's wife. Ordinarily she has a pleasant personality. Now, however, she is somewhat temperamental and excited because she is expecting a baby in two months. She had a tearful outburst soon after the group entered the shelter.

JIM   Is a minister. He is very easy-going and has remained calm and optimistic during the hours of waiting for the radio message. He has helped settle several arguments and helped to calm Donna when she cried. His presence is reassuring to the whole group.

JOE   Is a repairman. He is the only person without some college but he has a great deal of practical knowledge and can care for the air-filtration system. He is overweight and seems rather uninteresting. He sneaked a candy bar from the food supply, apparently unaware of or unconcerned about the necessity for self-control where food and water are concerned.

JOHN   Is a black basketball player, big and husky. The star center of his college team, he is highly respected by everyone on campus. Physically very strong, he was the only one able to lift the heavy metal plate that had to be put over the shelter door.

HELEN   Is a home economics major studying nutrition and dietetics. Her training makes her efficient (even domineering and bossy). Her first act was to assess the food supply. An imaginative cook, she could fix the shelter's food supply in an appealing way. She is also very sexy and attractive.

TIM   Is a musician who gets along well with everyone. His contagious smile, good sense of humor, and guitar playing have helped improve everyone's mood. He is attentive toward the girls and has offended Helen, who thinks he is being fresh.

Abigail River

I. Opening Prayer

Lord God of all creation, thank you for your goodness, your grace, your loving kindness, and your tender mercy. Help us to live our lives in your shadow and to show everyone your compassion through your love. Through Christ our Lord. Amen.

II. Business Report

III. Scripture Reading: Matthew 25:31–40

When the Son of Man comes in his glory, escorted by all the angels of heaven, he will sit upon his royal throne, and all the nations will be assembled before him. Then he will separate them into two groups, as a shepherd separates sheep from goats. The sheep he will place on his right hand, the goats on his left. The king will say to those on his right; "Come. You have my Father's blessing! Inherit the kingdom prepared for you from the creation of the world. For I was hungry and you gave me food, I was thirsty and you gave me drink. I was a stranger and you welcomed me, naked and you clothed me, in prison and you came to visit me." Then the just will ask him: "Lord, when did we see you hungry and feed you or see you thirsty and give you drink? When did we welcome you away from home or clothe you in your nakedness? When did we visit you when you were ill or in prison?" The king will answer them: "I assure you, as often as you did it for one of my least brothers you did it for me."

IV. Program

The program notes begin on the next page. You are encouraged to build on these ideas. However, each program is self-contained and can be used exactly as is if you desire. Refer to the section entitled "How To Use This Manual" for guidelines on conducting the program.

V. Closing Prayer

Lord, help us not to judge the actions of others, but to accept and love them as they have been created, in your image. Give us the insight, Lord, to see the good in those who have hurt us, and open our hearts to forgive and love all people as you have loved us. We ask this in your name. Amen.

A. Read the following story.

There was once a woman named Abigail who was in love with a man named Gregory. Gregory lived on the shore of a river, and Abigail lived on the opposite side. The river separating the two lovers was filled with man-eating alligators. Abigail wanted to cross the river to be with Gregory. Unfortunately, the bridge had been washed out. She went to Sinbad, the riverboat captain, and asked him to take her across the river. Sinbad replied that he would happily do so, but that first she must go to bed with him. Abigail promptly refused his offer, then went to a friend named Ivan to explain her plight. Ivan said that he did not want to be involved at all in the situation. Abigail then felt that her only choice was to accept Sinbad's terms. She went to bed with him; he then fulfilled his promise and took her across the river to Gregory. When Abigail told Gregory about her agreement with Sinbad, Gregory cast her aside. Heartsick and dejected, Abigail turned to Slug with her tale of woe. Slug, feeling compassion for Abigail, sought out Gregory and beat him brutally. This pleased Abigail. As the sun sets on the horizon, we see Abigail laughing at Gregory.

B. Rank the morality of the characters by writing their names on the lines below. Use 1 to denote the character you think is the best, 5 to denote the character you think is the worst.

1. _____

2. _____

3. _____

4. _____

5. _____

C. Break into small groups to discuss how you ranked the characters and why.

D. Answer the following questions:

1. After discussing the rankings with your group, do you feel like changing your rankings?

2. If you do want to change your rankings, why?

3. Did this activity give you any insight into the different ways that different people see the same situation?

Perception Triads

I. Opening Prayer

Dear heavenly Father, so often we call on you to give us guidance and direction. All the time we keep asking for help for our personal needs and desires. Often we do not think of others and their needs; often we do not surrender our will to you; often we do not act in obedience to your ideals. Yet you never forsake us; you are always ready to forgive us. In all humility, we pray tonight that you will clear the fog from our minds. Enable us to see ourselves truthfully as we really are, then show us truthfully how you want us to be. Help us to be a reflection of your love to all we meet, in all we do, and in all that we say or think. Amen.

II. Business Report

III. Scripture Reading: John 16:22–24

In the same way, you are sad for a time, but I shall see you again; then your heart will rejoice with a joy no one can take from you. On that day you will have no questions to ask me. I give you my assurance, whatever you ask the Father, he will give you in my name. Ask and you shall receive, that your joy may be full.

IV. Program

The program notes begin on the next page. You are encouraged to build on these ideas. However, each program is self-contained and can be used exactly as is if you desire. Refer to the section entitled "How To Use This Manual" for guidelines on conducting the program.

V. Closing Prayer

We thank you, Father, for your love; we wish that we could love as you do. Yet we accept our human nature, knowing that we will always fall short of your example. Help us to be open to others, to know no strangers, to accept all others as your beloved children. With your help, Lord, we seek for true and trusting friends, those who have sympathetic hearts and understanding minds. Amen.

A. Read the following list of adjectives, looking for the ones that describe you best.

proud	outgoing	vain
complex	rude	quiet
realistic	negative	idealistic
aggressive	blunt	prejudiced
mature	boastful	unfriendly
trusting	religious	liberal
happy	materialistic	confident
sincere	sensitive	open-minded
manipulative	fearful	stubborn
naive	selfish	studious
shy	sexy	wise
cheerful	trustworthy	free
sarcastic	energetic	conservative
warm	uptight	cool

B. Circle five adjectives from the list that you feel best describe you.

C. Count off by threes to form a triad. Mark five adjectives that describe each of the other members of your triad. (Use a different mark, underline, check, etc., for each person.)

D. Share your perceptions with one another. Try to account for the similarities and the differences. Discuss the following questions.

1. How do your perceptions compare with those in your triad?

2. What are the causes of the similarities and differences?

3. Can you learn anything new about yourself or your partners as a result of this activity? What?

4. What effect do differing perceptions have on interpersonal communication?

Fun In General

Minimum Level College Entrance Test

I. Opening Prayer

Lord, help us to let go of the crosses we bear. You have brought us together to be happy. Sometimes we need to stop and count your blessings, to smile, to laugh, and to play. Let us rejoice in your love of us. Amen.

II. Business Report

III. Scripture Reading: Jeremiah 31:12–14

Shouting, they shall mount the heights of Zion, they shall come streaming to the Lord's blessings: the grain, the wine, and the oil, the sheep and the oxen. They themselves shall be like watered gardens, never again shall they languish. Then the virgins shall make merry and dance, and young men and old as well. I will turn their mourning into joy, I will console and gladden them after their sorrows. I will lavish choice portions upon the priests, and my people shall be filled with my blessings, says the Lord.

IV. Program

The program notes begin on the next page. You are encouraged to build on these ideas. However, each program is self-contained and can be used exactly as is if you desire. Refer to the section entitled "How To Use This Manual" for guidelines on conducting the program.

V. Closing Prayer

Lord, you know that we humans resist change. You know that we fear the unknown. You know that being single is not always easy, whether or not it is by our choice. We need your loving guidance. Teach us how to create a rewarding and interesting life for ourselves. Help us learn to see and use the gifts you have given us. Through Christ our Lord. Amen.

ANSWER SHEET

NOTE TO PROGRAM LEADER: DO NOT DUPLICATE THIS SHEET. IT IS NOT TO BE PASSED OUT.

1. Sandbox	2. Man overboard
3. I understand	4. Reading between the lines
5. Long underwear	6. Crossroads
7. Downtown	8. Tricycle
9. Split-level	10. Three degrees below zero
11. Neon light	12. Circle under the eyes
13. High chair	14. Paradise
15. Touchdown	16. Six feet under ground
17. Mind over matter	18. He's beside himself
19. Backward glance	20. Life after death
21. Easy on the eyes	22. Mothballs
23. Black overcoat	24. Double-time
25. Shifting sands	26. Hurry up
27. Quit following me	28. Dark ages
29. Scrambled eggs	30. Uproar
31. Eggs over easy	32. Sock in the eye
33. Are you over 18	34. Spots before your eyes
35. Square meal	36. Look before you leap

MINIMAL LEVEL COLLEGE ENTRANCE TEST

Identify the following:

1 SAND (in box)	**2** MAN / BOARD	**3** STAND / I	**4** R/E/A/D/I/N/G
5 WEAR / LONG	**6** R ROAD A D	**7** T O W N	**8** CYCLE CYCLE CYCLE
9 LE VEL	**10** O / M.D. P.H.D. B.A.	**11** KNEE LIGHT	**12** ii ii / 0000000000000000000
13 CHAIR	**14** DICE DICE	**15** T O U C H	**16** GROUND / FEET FEET FEET FEET FEET FEET
17 MIND / MATTER	**18** HE'S / HIMSELF	**19** ECNALG	**20** DEATH LIFE
21 EZ / iiiiiiiiiiiiiiiiii	**22** MOTH (CRY, CRY, CRY)	**23** BLACK / COAT	**24** TIMETIME
25 S A N D S	**26** HURRY ↑	**27** ME QUIT	**28** AGES
29 GEGS EGSG GSGE GSEG	**30** ↑ ROAR	**31** EGGS / EASY	**32** I S O C K
33 RU / 18	**34** (dotted circle) iiiiiiiiii	**35** M E A L E A A E A E L A E M	**36** LOOK LEAP

· 163 ·

Think So?

I. Opening Prayer

Lord, I enjoy seeing the humor in myself and others. You have given us the gift of laughter to ease the stresses in our lives. Hold my hand and enjoy my happy times as you hold my hand when I am struggling. Let me not forget the innocence and joy of children so that I can become a stronger, happier person. Amen.

II. Business Report

III. Scripture Reading: Isaiah 35:1–4

The desert and the parched land will exult; the steppe will rejoice and bloom. They will bloom with abundant flowers, and rejoice with joyful song. The glory of Lebanon will be given to them, the splendor of Carmel and Sharon; they will see the glory of the Lord, the splendor of our God. Strengthen the hands that are feeble, make firm the knees that are weak. Say to those whose hearts are frightened: Be strong, fear not! Here is your God, he comes with vindication; with divine recompense he comes to save you.

IV. Program

The program notes begin on the next page. You are encouraged to build on these ideas. However, each program is self-contained and can be used exactly as is if you desire. Refer to the section entitled "How To Use This Manual" for guidelines on conducting the program.

V. Closing Prayer

Dear Lord, life can be serious, sad and lonely, or it can be joyous, full of laughter, warmth, and sharing. You have given us a choice about how we live our lives. Guide us to grow through the worst times so that we can enjoy the wholeness of new life. Amen.

DO NOT HAND THIS SHEET OUT—THIS IS A TIMED TEST. GIVE THE GROUP 10 MIN-UTES TO COMPLETE THE TEST.

Answers to the THINK SO? test.

1. YES. There is a July 4th and a July 5th, etc.

2. 1 (ONE). We only have one, but we celebrate it year after year.

3. No, not if he is LIVING.

4. The MATCH.

5. All twelve of the months have at least 28 days.

6. 1 hour. You take the first pill, then 1/2 hour later the second, then a 1/2 hour later the third.

7. White. A polar bear!

8. HALF-WAY, then he is running out.

9. 10, nine plus the batter. 6, three for each side.

10. Fifty cent piece, and a nickel. ONE is not a nickel, but the other one is a nickel.

11. 17. He HAS 17, but eight are dead.

12. 70. 30 DIVIDED by 1/2 equals 60, plus 10.

13. They played different opponents.

14. 2 apples, the two you took.

15. IMPOSSIBLE, how could you date a coin B.C. (Before Christ) if you did not know Christ was coming or when he was coming.

16. They would not bury the SURVIVORS anywhere.

17. The beggar is a woman. They are sisters.

18. None, MOSES did not have an ark it was Noah's Ark.

19. It is impossible because he is deceased.

20. None, you cannot get anything out of an existing hole.

21. 3, at least two would have to be the same color.

22. 99 plus 9/9.

23. Push the cork into the bottle.

24. You cannot dig HALF a hole.

25. He can go to bed in the daytime.

26. The doctor is the son's MOTHER.

27. CANADA; the rest of the time you will be over water.

28. 12; there are always twelve in a dozen.

29. United States of America.

30. Neither, seven and eight equal FIFTEEN not thirteen.

31. 3 minutes. It takes 3 minutes for each cat to kill a rat.

DISCUSSION QUESTIONS FOR THE GROUP:

1. Were you surprised at how many questions you could not answer?

2. Were you surprised at how many questions you answered correctly or incorrectly?

3. What did this test tell you about the assumptions you make?

4. Does this activity tell you anything about what misinformation can be derived from not really listening?

Think So Quiz

Purpose: To discover fallacies of thinking based on hidden assumptions and over-generalizations.

Procedure: This is a timed test. Answer the questions as quickly as possible. Once you have answered, go on to the next question. DO NOT GO BACK TO CHANGE ANY ANSWERS.

1. Each country has its own "Independence Day." Do they have a 4th of July in England?

2. How many birthdays does the average man have?

3. Can a man living in Winston-Salem, North Carolina be buried west of the Mississippi?

4. If you only had one match and entered a room in which there was a kerosene lamp, an oil heater and a wood burning stove, which would you light first and why?

5. Some months have 30 days, some have 31. How many have 28?

6. If a doctor gave you 3 pills and told you to take one every half-hour, how long would the pills last?

7. A house is built so that each side has a southern exposure. If a bear were to wander by the house, what most likely would the color of the bear be?

8. How far can a dog run into the forest?

9. What is the minimum number of active baseball players on the field during any part of an inning? How many outs in an inning?

10. I have in my hand two U.S. coins that total 55 cents in value. One is not a nickel. What are the two coins?

11. A farmer has 17 sheep. All but 9 died. How many does he have left?

12. Divide 30 by one-half and add 10. What's the answer?

13. Two men play chess. They played five games and each man won the same number of games. There were no ties. How can this be?

14. Take two apples from three apples and what do you get?

15. An archaeologist claimed he found gold coins dated 46 B.C. Do you think he did, and why?

16. An airplane crashed exactly on the U.S.-Mexican border. Where would they bury the survivors?

17. A woman gives a beggar 50 cents. The woman is the beggar's sister, but the beggar is not the woman's brother. How can this be?

18. How many animals of each species did Moses take aboard the ark with him?

19. Is it legal in California for a man to marry his widow's sister?

20. How much dirt may be removed from a hole that is 6 feet deep, 2 feet wide, and 10 feet long?

21. If your bedroom were pitch dark and you needed a matching pair of socks, how many socks would you need to take out of the bureau drawer if there are 25 white and 25 blue socks in the drawer?

22. You have four nines (9,9,9,9). Arrange them to total 100. You may use any of the arithmetical processes (addition, subtraction, multiplication, or division). Each nine can be used only once.

23. You have a dime in an otherwise empty wine bottle. The bottle is corked. Your job is to get the dime out of the bottle without taking the cork out. You cannot damage the bottle. How would you do this?

24. If it takes 10 men ten days to dig a hole, how long will it take 5 men to dig half a hole?

25. Explain the following boast: "In my bedroom, the nearest lamp that I usually keep turned on is 20 feet away from my bed. Alone in the room, without using any special devices, I can turn out the light on the lamp and get into bed before the room is dark." How can he do this?

26. A doctor refuses to operate on a patient who has been injured in an auto accident in which the

patient's father was killed. The doctor refuses to operate because the patient is the doctor's son. How can this be?

27. You are living in Detroit, Michigan. If you travel due south, what is the first foreign country you will enter?

28. There are 12 one-cent stamps in a dozen, but how many two-cent stamps are there in a dozen?

29. What four words appear on every denomination of U.S. coin and currency?

30. Which is correct: Seven and eight IS thirteen, or Seven and eight ARE thirteen?

31. If three cats kill three rats in three minutes, how long will it take for 100 cats to kill 100 rats?

Appendix

Reading List (Listed alphabetically by title)

About Dying, Sara B. Stein. 1984, Walker & Co.

Al(exandra) the Great, Constance C. Greene. 1982, Viking Child Books.

And You Give Me a Pain, Elaine, Stella Persner. 1979, Houghton Mifflin.

Animal, the Vegetable and John D. Jones, Betsy Byars. 1983, Dell.

Annulment, Joseph P. Zuack. 1983, Harper & Row.

Annulments, Lawrence G. Wrenn. 1988, Cannon Law Society.

Art of Loving, Erich Fromm. 1989, Harper Collins.

Bear's House, Marilyn Sachs. 1987, Dutton Child Books.

Beatitudes: Soundings in Christian Traditions, Simon Tugwell. 1980, Templegate.

Boy Who Wanted a Family, Shirley Gordon. 1982, Dell.

Boys & Girls Book About Divorce, Richard A. Gardner. 1971, Bantam.

Boys & Girls Book About One-Parent Families, Richard A. Gardner. 1983, Creative Therapeutics.

Boys & Girls Book About Step Families, Richard A. Gardner. 1985, Creative Therapeutics.

Breaking Up, Norma Klein. 1980, Pantheon.

By Death or Divorce: It Hurts To Lose, Amy R. Mumford. 1981, Accent Books.

Called To Be Friends, Paula Ripple. 1980, Ave Maria.

Caring Question: You First or Me First? Choosing a Healthy Balance, Donald A. Tubesing and Nancy L. Tubesing. 1983, Augsburg Fortress.

Cat Called Camouflage, Cordelia Jones. 1971, S.G. Phillips.

Catholics & Broken Marriages, John T. Catoir. 1979, Ave Maria.

Centering Prayer, M. Basil Pennington. 1982, Doubleday.

Challenge of Marriage, Rudolf Dreikurs. 1978, NAL-Dutton.

Children of Divorce, Louise J. Despert. 1963, Doubleday.

Children of Parting Parents, Lora H. Tessman. 1978, Aronson Inc.

Christian Life Patterns, Evelyn E. Whitehead and James D. Whitehead. 1982, Doubleday.

Compassion: A Reflection on Christian Life, Donald McNeill. 1983, Doubleday.

Compassionate Side of Divorce, C.S. Lovett. 1975, Christianity.

Contact: The First Four Minutes, Leonard Zunin and Natalie Zunin. 1986, Ballantine.

Contemplative Prayer, Thomas Merton. 1989, Doubleday.

Creative Divorce, Mel Krantzler. 1975, NAL-Dutton.

Creative Intimacy, Jerry Greenwald. 1984, Jove Publications.

Daily We Touch Him, M. Basil Pennington. 1977, Doubleday.

Dark But Full of Diamonds, Letcher C. Lyle. 1981, Putnam's.

Dear Lola: How To Build Your Own Family, Judie Angell. 1986, Dell.

Death: The Final Stage of Growth, Elisabeth Kübler-Ross. 1975, Prentice-Hall.

Divorce and Remarriage in the Catholic Church, Gerald D. Coleman. 1988, Paulist Press.

Divorce Ministry and the Marriage Tribunal, James J. Young. 1982, Paulist Press.

Do I Have a Daddy? Jeanne W. Lindsay. 1991, Morning Glory.

Don't Make Me Smile, Barbara Park. 1981, Knopf.

Egypt Game, Zilpha K. Snyder. 1986, Dell.

Explaining Death to Children, Earl A. Grollman. 1969, Beacon.

Family Crucible, Augustus Y. Napier and Carl A. Whitaker. 1984, Bantam.

Father Every Few Years, Alice Bach. 1977, Harper Colophon Child Books.

Friendship Factor: How To Get Closer to the People You Care For, Alan L. McGinnis. 1979, Augsburg Fortress.

Fully Human, Fully Alive, John Powell. 1989, Tabor.

Gift of the Pirate Queen, Patricia R. Giff. 1983, Dell.

Girl Called Al, Constance C. Greene. 1977, Dell.

Going It Alone: The Family Life & Social Situation of the Single Parent, Robert S. Weiss. 1981, Basic.

Good-bye, Chicken Little, Betsy Byars. 1990, Harper Colophon Child Books.

Growing Through Divorce, Jim Smoke. 1986, Bantam.

Guide to Non-Sexist Children's Books, Vol. II: 1976–1985, Denise Wilms and Ilene Cooper. 1987, Academy Chi Publications.

Hand Me Another Brick, Charles R. Swindoll. 1983, Bantam.

He Leadeth Me, Walter J. Ciszek and Daniel L. Flaherty. 1975, Doubleday.

Headless Cupid, Zilpha K. Snyder. 1985, Dell.

Heal My Heart, O Lord, Joan Hutson. 1976, Ave Maria.

Healing Life's Hurts: Healing Memories Through the Five Stages of Forgiveness, Dennis Linn and Matthew Linn. 1978, Paulist Press.

Helping Hand, James L. Horstman and Van T. Moon. 1993, Paulist Press.

How To Be Your Own Best Friend, Mildred Newman and Bernard Berkowitz. 1986, Ballantine.

How To Fall Out of Love, Debora Phillips and Robert Judd. 1984, Warner Books.

How To Father, Fitzhugh Dodson. 1975, NAL-Dutton.

How To Get Control of Your Time and Your Life, Alan Lakein. 1989, NAL-Dutton.

How To Get It Together When Your Parents Are Coming Apart, Arlene Richards and Irene Willis. Willard Press.

How To Listen Assertively, Baxter Geeting & Corinne Geeting. 1982, International Semantics.

How To Parent, Fitzhugh Dodson. 1971, NAL-Dutton.

How To Survive the Loss of a Love, Melba Colgrove. 1984, Bantam.

Human Relations and Your Career, David W. Johnson. 1990, Prentice-Hall

I Know You, Al, Constance C. Greene. 1977, Dell.

I Love My Mother, Paul Zindel. 1975, Harper Colophon Child Books.

I, Trissy, Norman F. Mazer. 1986, Dell.

Impact of Divorce on the Extended Family, Esther O. Fisher. 1982, Haworth.

Inward Stillness, George Maloney. 1989, Dimension Books.

It's Not the End of the World, Judy Blume. 1982, Macmillan.

Joining Together: Group Theory and Group Skills, David Johnson and Frank Johnson. 1991, Prentice-Hall.

Joshua's Day, Sandra L. Surowiecki. 1977, Lollipop Power.

Julie of the Wolves, Jean C. George. 1972, Harper Colophon Child Books.

Kid's Book of Divorce: By, for and About Kids, Eric Rofes. 1982, Random House.

Learing To Love Again: Beyond Creative Divorce, Mel Krantzler. 1979, Bantam.

Letters from the Desert, Carlo Carretto. 1982, Orbis Books.

Limbo World of the Divorced, James J. Rue and Louise Shanahan. 1979, Franciscan Herald.

Listening Made Easy, Robert L. Montgomery. 1984, AMACOM.

Living Alone and Liking It, Lynn Shahan. 1982, Warner Books.

Living Prayer, Metropolitan A. Bloom. 1975, Templegate.

Living with Death and Dying, Elisabeth Kübler-Ross. 1979, Macmillan.

Loneliness Is for Loving, Robert E. Lauder. 1988, Living Flame Press.

Mama, Lee B. Hopkins. 1978, Dell.

Marital Separation: Managing After a Marriage Ends, Robert S. Weiss. 1975, Basic Books.

Martin's Father, Margrit Eichler. 1977, Lollipop Power.

Masquerade, Susan Shreve. 1981, Dell.

Merton's Place of Nowhere, James Finley. 1978, Ave Maria.

Mirages of Marriage, William J. Leder and Don D. Jackson. 1990, Norton.

Mitzi and the Terrible Tyrannosaurus Rex, Barbara Williams. 1982, NAL-Dutton.

Mom, the Wolfman and Me, Norma Klein. 1972, Pantheon.

Mommies at Work, Eve Merriam. 1991, S&S Trade.

Monastic Journey, Thomas Merton. 1978, Doubleday.

Mother Teresa: Her Work and Her People, Desmond Doig. 1980, Harper.

Mr. and Mrs. Bo Jo Jones, Ann Head. 1968, NAL-Dutton.

Night Swimmers, Betsy Byars. 1983, Dell.

No More Secrets for Me, Oralee Wachter. 1984, Little Brown.

On Children and Death, Elisabeth Kübler-Ross. 1985, Macmillan.

On Death and Dying, Elisabeth Kübler-Ross. 1970, Macmillan.

Out of Solitude, Henri J. Nouwen. 1974, Ave Maria.

Pain and the Possibility, Paula Ripple. 1978, Ave Maria.

Parents Book About Divorce, Richard Gardner. 1991, Bantam.

Pastoral Care and Counseling in Grief and Separation, Wayne E. Oates. 1976, Augsburg Fortress.

People Skills, Robert Bolton. 1986, S&S Trade.

Pinballs, Betsy Byars. 1987, Harper Colophon Child Books.

Pippi Longstocking, Astrid Lindgren. 1988, Puffin Books.

Planet of Junior Brown, Virginia Hamilton. 1986, Macmillan.

Poustinia, Catherine Doherty. 1975, Ave Maria.

Poverty of Spirit, Johannes B. Metz. 1968, Paulist Press.

Prayer Is a Hunger, Edward Farrell. 1972, Dimension Books.

Prayer: Living With God, Simon Tugwell. 1980, Templegate.

Prayer of the Heart, George A. Maloney. 1981, Ave Maria.

Prayers, Michel Quoist. 1985, Sheed & Ward.

Rainbow Jordan, Alice Childress. 1982, Avon.

Rainbow Kid, Jeanne Belancourt. 1983, Avon.

Reaching Out, Henri J. Nouwen. 1985, Walker & Co.

Reaching Out: Interpersonal Effectiveness and Self Actualization, David W. Johnson. 1986, Prentice-Hall.

Rebuilding: When Your Relationship Ends, Bruce Fisher. 1981, Impact.

Remember the Secret, Elisabeth Kübler-Ross. 1988, Celestial Arts.

Road Less Traveled, M. Scott Peck. 1988, S&S.

Robbie and the Leap Year Blues, Norma Klein. 1990, Knopf.

Ronnie and Rosey, Judie Angell. 1979, Dell.

Sadhana: A Way to God, Anthony De Mello. 1984, Doubleday.

Sam, Bangs and Moonshine, Evaline Ness. 1966, Holt.

Season In-Between, Jan Greenberg. 1979, Farrar, Strauss and Giroux.

Seasons of a Man's Life, Daniel J. Levinson. 1986, Ballantine.

Secret Lives, Berthe Amoss. 1981, Dell.

Secret of Staying in Love: Loving Relationships Through Communication, John Powell. 1990, Tabor.

Self-Esteem, Virginia Satir. 1975, Celestial Arts.

Servant Leadership: A Journey into the Nature of Legitimate Power and Greatness, Robert K. Greenleaf. 1977, Paulist Press.

Single-Parent Family in Children's Books: An Annotated Bibliography, Catherine T. Horner. 1988, Scarecrow.

Small Group Decision Making, B. Aubrey Fisher. 1990, McGraw-Hill.

Spirituality and the Gentle Life, Adrian Van Kaam. 1990, Dimension.

Star for the Latecomer, Bonnie Zindel and Paul Zindel. 1980, Harper Colophon Child Books.

Straight Talk: A New Way To Get Close to Others by Saying What You Really Mean, Sherod Miller. 1982, NAL-Dutton.

Suddenly Single: Learning To Start Over, A Personal Guide, John Robertson and Betty Utterback. 1986, S&S.

Sweet Whispers, Brother Rush, Virginia Hamilton. 1982, Putnam.

Talking About Death: A Dialogue Between Parent and Child, Earl A. Grollman. 1991, Beacon.

Talking About Divorce and Separation: A Dialogue Between Parent and Child, Earl A. Grollman. 1988, Beacon.

That Man Is You, Louis Evely. 1964, Paulist Press.

This Is a Recording: Listening with a Purpose, Barbara F. Swartz and Richard L. Smith. 1986, Prentice-Hall.

Through a Brief Darkness, Richard Peck. 1989, Dell.

Tiger Eyes, Judy Blume. 1982, Dell.

Tina Gogo, Judie Angell. 1980, Dell.

Toby Lived Here, Hilma Wolitzer. 1978, Farrar, Straus and Giroux.

Toddlers and Parents, T. Berry Brazelton. 1989, Doubleday.

Transformation of Man, Rosemary Haughton. 1980, Templegate.

Transitions: Making Sense of Life's Changes, William Bridges. 1980, Addison-Wesley.

Two Homes To Live In: A Child's Eye View of Divorce, Barbara S. Hazen. 1978, Human Sciences Press.

Walking with Loneliness, Paula Ripple. 1982, Ave Maria.

What Shall We Tell the Kids? Bennett Olshaker. 1989, Lynx.

What's Best for You? Judie Angell. 1983, Dell.

When My Dad Died: A Child's View of Death, Janice M. Hammond. 1981, Cranbrook.

When My Mommy Died: A Child's View of Death, Janice M. Hammond. 1980, Cranbrook.

When Someone Asks for Help: A Practical Guide to Counseling, Everett L. Worhtington, Jr. 1982, InterVarsity.

When the Well Runs Dry: Prayer Beyond the Beginnings, Thomas H. Green. 1979, Ave Maria.

Where Is Daddy? The Story of a Divorce, Beth Godd. 1969, Beacon.

Where the Lilies Bloom, Vera Cleaver and Bill Cleaver. 1969, Harper Colophon Child Books.

Who, Me Lead a Group? Jean I. Clarke. 1985, Harper.

Why Am I Afraid To Tell You Who I Am? John Powell. 1990, Tabor.

Why Do I Think I Am Nothing Without a Man? Penelope Russianoff. 1985, Bantam.

Wisdom of Insecurity, Alan W. Watts. 1968, Random House.

With Open Hands, Henri J. Nouwen. 1972, Ave Maria.

Words To Love By, Mother Teresa. 1983, Ave Maria.

Working Parents Survival Guide, Sally W. Olds. 1989, Prima.

Wounded Healer: Ministry in Contemporary Society, Henri J. Nouwen. 1979, Doubleday.

Your Child's Self-Esteem: The Key to His Life, Dorothy C. Briggs. 1975, Doubleday.

Your Many Faces, Virginia Satir. 1978, Celestial Arts.

Your Old Pal, Al, Constance C. Greene. 1981, Dell.